MERTON & WALSH ON THE PERSON

By Dr. Robert Imperato

WIPF & STOCK · Eugene, Oregon

Wipf and Stock Publishers
199 W 8th Ave, Suite 3
Eugene, OR 97401

Merton and Walsh on the Person
By Imperato, Robert L.
Copyright©1987 by Imperato, Robert L.
ISBN 13: 978-1-4982-0227-5
Publication date 8/19/2014
Previously published by Liturgical Press, 1987

ACKNOWLEDGMENTS

Excerpt from *Plotinus*, by A. H. Armstrong, copyright 1953; reprinted by permission of Allen & Unwin, London.

Excerpts from *Bernard of Clairvaux: Treatises II*, copyright 1980, *The Climate of Monastic Prayer*, by Thomas Merton, copyright 1969, *The Monastic Theology of Aelred of Rivaulx*, by A. Hallier, copyright 1969, and *Thomas Merton on St. Bernard*, by Thomas Merton, copyright 1980; reprinted by permission of Cistercian Publications, Kalamazoo, Michigan 49008.

Excerpts from *Confessions of a Guilty Bystander*, by Thomas Merton, copyright 1965, 1966 by the Abbey of Gethsemani; reprinted by permission of Doubleday & Co., Inc. Excerpts from *Contemplation in a World of Action*, by Thomas Merton, copyright 1965, 1969, 1970, 1971 by the Trustees of the Merton Legacy Trust; reprinted by permission of Doubleday & Co., Inc.

Excerpts from "The Inner Experience," by Thomas Merton, "Conference on Prayer," by Thomas Merton, and *Redeeming the Time*, by Thomas Merton; reprinted by permission of The Merton Legacy Trust.

Excerpt from "Concerning the Collection in the Bellarmine College Library," by Thomas Merton, reprinted by permission of the Thomas Merton Studies Center, Bellarmine College, Louisville, Kentucky 40205.

Excerpts from the following books by Thomas Merton are reprinted by permission of the New Directions Publishing Corp., New York 10014: *Asian Journal*, copyright 1973 by The Trustees of the Merton Legacy Trust; *Collected Poems*, copyright 1977 by The Trustees of the Merton Legacy Trust; *My Argument with the Gestapo*, copyright 1969 by the Abbey of Gethsemani, Inc.; *New Seeds of Contemplation* (and the original, *Seeds*) copyright 1961 by the Abbey of Gethsemani, Inc.; *Raids on the Unspeakable*, copyright 1964 by New Directions Publishing Corporation; and *Zen and the Birds of Appetite*, copyright 1968 by the Abbey of Gethsemani, Inc.

Thomas Merton, Monk, ed. by Patrick Hart, used with permission of Sheed & Ward, 115 E. Armour Blvd., Box 281, Kansas City, Missouri 64141-0281.

Excerpt from "Merton's Peacemaking," by James H. Forest, Dec. 1978; reprinted with permission from *Sojourners*, Box 29272, Washington, D.C. 20017.

Reprinted by Farrar, Straus & Giroux, Inc.: excerpt from *Disputed Questions*, by Thomas Merton, copyright 1953, 1959, 1960 by the Abbey of Our Lady of Gethsemani; excerpts from *The Secular Journal*, by Thomas Merton, copyright 1959 by Madonna House and reprinted by Farrar, Straus & Giroux, Inc.; excerpts from *Mystics and Zen Masters*, by Thomas Merton, copyright 1961, 1962, 1964, 1965, 1966, 1967 by the Abbey of Gethsemani and reprinted by permission of Farrar, Straus & Giroux, Inc.

Excerpt from *The Last of the Fathers*, by Thomas Merton, copyright 1948 by Harcourt Brace Jovanovich, Inc. (renewed in 1976 by The Trustees of the Merton Legacy Trust); reprinted by permission of the publisher.

Excerpts from *The Seven Storey Mountain*, by Thomas Merton, copyright 1948 by Harcourt Brace Jovanovich, Inc., and renewed in 1976 by The Trustees of the Merton Legacy Trust; reprinted by permission of the publisher.

Excerpt from *The Waters of Siloe*, copyright 1949 by Rev. M. Louis (Thomas Merton) and renewed in 1977 by The Trustees of the Merton Legacy Trust; reprinted by permission of Harcourt Brace Jovanovich, Inc.

Excerpt from *The Sign of Jonas*, by Thomas Merton, copyright 1953 by the Abbey of Our Lady of Gethsemani and renewed in 1981 by The Trustees of the Merton Legacy Trust; reprinted by permission of Harcourt Brace Jovanovich, Inc.

LIST OF ABBREVIATIONS

The following abbreviations are used for works by Thomas Merton that are frequently cited in this book.

AJ	*The Asian Journal*
CGB	*Confessions of a Guilty Bystander*
CMP	*The Climate of Monastic Prayer*
CP	*Contemplative Prayer*
CWA	*Contemplation in a World of Action*
IE	"The Inner Experience"
LL	*Love and Living*
MZM	*Mystics and Zen Masters*
NM	*The New Man*
NS	*New Seeds of Contemplation*
NVA	*The Nonviolent Alternative*
SC	*Seeds of Contemplation*
SJ	*The Sign of Jonas*
WS	*The Waters of Siloe*
ZBA	*Zen and the Birds of Appetite*

CONTENTS

I. Why This Book? 1

II. The Theological Context 13

III. Personhood according to Walsh 59

IV. Merton and Walsh 89

V. The Key to Merton's Thought 119

VI. The Significance for
Christian Thought 147

    Bibliography 157

I

WHY THIS BOOK?

THE MAIN PURPOSE of this study is to examine the notion of the person according to Daniel Clark Walsh and Thomas Merton. For both of these thinkers, person is a central notion — one on which they are essentially in agreement. An understanding of this link between Walsh and Merton opens up the metaphysical depths of Merton's thought. But as person is a metaphysical notion, there arises the danger of undue abstractness. Merton tries to guard against an overly abstract understanding of person. In so doing, he moves beyond Walsh's thought by clearly acknowledging that the individual human nature is the vehicle for expressing the person.

For both men, personhood is a relationship with God that originates in God's intimacy with Himself. Though person is clearly at the heart of Walsh's thought, the notion of the person also provides a unifying theme for Merton's varied writings and concerns. The person-centered thought of Walsh and Merton emerges from their efforts to write about God-centered living; in harmony with their efforts, I offer an analysis of their thought on the person from within the context of Christian spirituality.

Two basic understandings of person are mentioned in this book. One categorizes person as a type of being relative to other types. This approach holds the human person to be an individual and rational substance.[1] The other approach, illustrated in the writings of Walsh and Merton, sees person as image of God. The former approach attempts to refine the definition of person and to categorize person as a type of object, a "what." The latter seeks to contextualize person in relation to God, for persons originate in God and are called to union with Him. Person in this sense is the ground of each human being's theological identity.

I first heard Daniel Clark Walsh when he was addressing a group of novices at the Abbey of Gethsemani in 1969. I was a member of that novitiate and listened intently. Unfortunately, I was unable to understand very much. Over the years as a novice and junior at Gethsemani, I found that the focus of Walsh's interest became my own. Walsh became a friend in the years preceding his death in 1975. Through our friendship and through monastic living, I became fascinated with one idea: the person as loving relationship with God. This idea is sufficiently deep to be capable of unifying much of life.

In the monastery on Sunday evenings, I used to take the supper trays to Fr. John the Baptist, an octogenarian monk confined to the infirmary. I would sit and talk with him, and nearly every week he would tell me the same thing: "If God didn't love me, I wouldn't exist." I reasoned that though much of his memory had slipped away and his mind was not cluttered by information that people regard as timely, he nevertheless had a central idea that brought profound meaning to his years of restriction to the infirmary. That idea, which had penetrated his everyday life, had enormous power to unify his experience.

When Fr. John the Baptist would look back over his more than eighty years, he would often ask, "Where did it all go?" His question referred to all of the events, thoughts, images, and feelings that make up the richness of daily life. John the Baptist's life of prayer had given him an orientation partially expressed by a few basic insights into life. Thomas Merton and his teacher and friend Daniel Walsh found a similar unifying principle, the person, which this book explores.

Walsh's sometimes meandering method of teaching, which involved his circling around the notion of person while his listeners gradually focussed their understanding, was particularly well suited to a monastic setting. At Gethsemani, the monks had no fear of tests to drive them to fill notebooks. One monk told me that he had listened to Walsh for five years before really understanding what he was talking about! Walsh's person-centered thought can be conceptualized in a short time, but to have that insight sew together the many patches of one's Christian existence requires a developmental preparation beyond intellectual readiness.

For those privileged to learn from Walsh, the notion of person becomes a therapeutic insight. By "therapeutic insight," I mean one that challenges and deepens self-understanding and invites unification of one's experience.

Walsh's famous student, Thomas Merton, allowed the notion of the person to touch his own center. He also protected this notion from undue abstraction and took it into the realms of social justice and dialog with Oriental spirituality. The notion of the person is never far from the pages of Thomas Merton.

Scholarly Oversight

MERTON SCHOLARS have consistently overlooked the influence of Merton and Walsh on each other. To those familiar with life at Gethsemani and with Merton's intellectual development, this oversight is difficult to justify. Two recent books on Merton illustrate the scholarly oversight of Walsh's influence. Shannon's *Thomas Merton's Dark Path*,[2] a book that deals with Merton's inner experience, does not include Walsh in the index. Commentators often follow Merton's *Seven Storey Mountain* and note that Walsh was Merton's trusted teacher at Columbia University whom he sought out when he was trying to decide about becoming a priest.[3] They also note that Walsh's conversation with Merton led to Merton's initial contact with Gethsemani.

Perhaps Shannon skips over the now-standard acknowledgment of Walsh's influence on Merton's vocational search while he was attending Columbia because Shannon does not focus on Merton's life but only on his thought. Those who knew Walsh know that he had a profound influence on Merton's thought as well as on his early vocational decision.

Richard Cashen, in his *Solitude in the Thought of Thomas Merton*,[4] comes closer than Shannon to recognizing the sources of Merton's person-centered thought. Apparently basing his judgment on passing references in *The Seven Storey Mountain*, Cashen gives vague acknowledgment of the influence on Merton of E. Gilson, J. Maritain, Walsh, and scholastic theology.[5] The depth and extent of the Walsh influence need to be brought to light if the unity of Merton's thought is to be understood.

Shannon briefly writes of thoughts on the true self of Merton's *New Seeds of Contemplation* and concludes that the distinctions between person and individual probably come from the influence of Maritain.[6] Walsh in fact acknowledges in print, in 1969, what Shannon asserts: that "from Maritain Merton borrowed the distinctions between the notions of individual, the common or communal good, and the person in man." Walsh continues, however, in such a way as to point beyond Maritain: "Merton's development of these topics is along less philosophical lines and more spiritual directions."[7]

Six years later, Walsh rejects attributing to Maritain Merton's meaning of person. In 1975, Fr. Flavian Burns, OCSO, who had been Merton's confessor and last abbot and who probably knew Merton on the spiritual level better than anyone else, asked Walsh, who knew Merton better than anyone else on the intellectual level, about the writers of theses saying that Merton's concepts of self and the deeper self had been gleaned from Maritain. "Oh!" Walsh responded, "It's far from that."[8]

Merton's personalistic thought goes beyond the philosophical distinctions of Maritain; Merton offers a person-centered spirituality, which is a focus of this book. But more important than sources and influences is the insight into the meaning of person that was held by Walsh and Merton. This insight provides a unifying key to the breadth and depth of Merton's thought.

Merton scholars have relied too heavily on published sources to have discovered the profound influence of Walsh, who published very little. The only two commentators to acknowledge Walsh's influence on Merton are Finley and Distefano.[9] Both knew Walsh at Gethsemani and know the importance of Walsh in his own right and in relation to Merton. Unfortunately, both Finley's and Distefano's references to Walsh are extremely brief, and neither provides a detailed study of Walsh's language or of his influence on Merton.

Sources

TO EXPRESS WALSH'S THOUGHT on the person, I have relied heavily upon his published and unpublished papers, which are collected at the Abbey of Gethsemani. These papers include Walsh's doctoral dissertation and several papers on philosophical topics.[10] Most of these papers stem from talks he gave to the monks at Gethsemani, where Walsh helped in the priestly formation of the monks by teaching philosophy.

When Walsh worked at Gethsemani in the 1960s, the Trappist Cistercians had been accustomed to ordaining a large percentage of their men to the priesthood. Although in the late 1960s this habit was changing, Walsh taught at Gethsemani when there was still strong demand for philosophical formation as part of priestly training. In the years when Walsh offered such standard courses as philosophy of man and metaphysics, he nevertheless became identified in the minds of the monks as one who taught on the person. This identification grew out of Walsh's courses to the student monks, or "scholastics," as well as to the entire community in "chapter talks."

The Rule of St. Benedict institutes gatherings within the monastery for spiritual teaching; these teachings, or chapter talks, are usually given by the abbot. Several chapter talks given by Walsh have been preserved and transcribed. When these talks have no title, I use their date as identification and adhere to the list in the Walsh file at Gethsemani for the convenience of other scholars. The simplicity of these brief chapter talks makes them more accessible than Walsh's lengthier papers.

Walsh's longer and more technical papers on the person come from his talks at the neighboring seminary at St. Mary's, Kentucky, and at St. Meinrad's Benedictine Abbey, St. Meinrad, Indiana. Other vital sources for Walsh's teaching on the person are dialogs between himself and several monks and friends that were held at Gethsemani late in Walsh's life. These dialogs are especially helpful in that the reader can benefit from the efforts of others to elicit clarifications from Walsh.

Finally, there are several tapes at Gethsemani on which Walsh speaks of personhood. The only other secondary sources in addition to Distefano's short article are Walsh's former students, several of whom meet at Gethsemani annually to discuss Walsh's thought.

The Merton sources are easier to obtain, since all published and unpublished works as well as works about him are assembled at the Merton Studies Center, Bellarmine College, Louisville, Kentucky.

The books of Bailey, Baker, Higgins, Malits, Padovano, and Shannon are insightful, but these writers do not speak about the notion of the person that Walsh and Merton jointly developed.[11] At most, these books mention the true versus false self-polarity but do not refer to Walsh or to person language. In one master's degree thesis, "Thomas Merton and the Image of Man," by Alvin W. Hergott,[12] there is passing reference to confusion between person and individual. Hergott is to be congratulated for acknowledging the distinction, but he does not explain it.

The secondary sources on Merton have been helpful chiefly in confirming that the meaning of person according to Walsh and Merton has not yet been explored. I thus rely upon primary sources in discussing Merton's understanding of person. For the reader's sake, I have attempted to use published works and those in current editions whenever possible. Occasionally I must refer to unpublished works of Merton, especially "The Inner Experience,"[13] which however has been published serially in the journal *Cistercian Studies* from 1983-1984.

Method and Structure

MERTON'S DEVELOPMENT OF THE NOTION of the person is properly appreciated within the overall context of his theology, in which the person is a unifying key. What Walsh and Merton contribute to Christian thought is a wedding of person language with image-of-God language. Merton's theological anthropology emerges from his Cistercian roots in addition to his dialog with Walsh. To be faithful to Merton's theological context, in chapter two, I examine his classical theological framework, namely creation, or origin, in the image of God, fall into unlikeness, and return to God in Christ by self-transcendence. Although the use of such polarities as person versus individual in later chapters will clarify the notion of the person, persons do not exist in a vacuum. This theological drama of origin, fall, and return adequately contextualizes his meaning of person.

There is a tendency, typified by Edward Rice in his unauthorized biography of Merton, *Man in the Sycamore Tree*,[14] to refer to exotic influences on Merton. Instead chapter two makes references to Merton's reliance upon twelfth-century Cistercians, especially Bernard of Clairvaux. One may easily conclude from chapter two that Merton's cultural identity is deeply affected by his own Cistercian tradition.

For Merton, humans fall from likeness to God into exteriority; that is, people lose inner peace. Loss of security or stability in God leads to self-preoccupation and self-assertion, which are part of fallenness. The return to God involves a transformation of psychological identity, in which one is stripped of illusion by dread and brought into freedom from self-justifying efforts. This is the freedom of one who is loved by God. Chapter two explores the inner path to God and others versus the way of isolated introversion.

The history of the notion of the person shows "relation" to be a central component of that notion. Relation is inherently difficult to define, as its meaning derives from the terms of the relationship. Fatherhood, for example, is a relationship that consists in having offspring; it is not definable in isolation from offspring.

A definition seeks to state what a person is, but Merton and Walsh feel that whatness, or essence, is a different dimension from the personal, the *who* one is. Another important term that emerges in the history of the notion of person, especially from Richard of St. Victor and Duns Scotus, is *incommunicability*. Chapter three will show Walsh's use of the terms *relation* and *incommunicable* and his focus on *who* rather than *what* a person is.

Chapter three attempts for the first time systematically to present Walsh's insight into the meaning of person. Walsh locates the origin of personhood in God's incommunicable experience of Himself as imitable. God's incommunicability thus grounds human uniqueness. Since Walsh does not want people to confuse personal life with individualism, he does not give much development to the concept of human uniqueness.

It is characteristic of Walsh to communicate his thought through pairs of linked concepts, such as person and nature, person and individual, individuality and uniqueness. Within these polarities is a tension between the concepts of person and individual, which are commonly assumed to be synonymous terms. This tension challenges our ordinary self-understanding, and such challenges were part of Walsh's method of teaching. As transformation of self is a common theme within spirituality, so that portion of Walsh's often abstract writing that offers challenge to self-understanding rightly belongs within the realm of spirituality. The issue of person versus community is also explored, and Walsh sees Christian community rooted in what all share: relationship with God. Walsh contrasts his view with a focus on personality differences, or what distinguishes people from one another.

Chapter four shows that Merton and Walsh have equivalent understandings of the notion of the person. The same polarities of person versus nature, person and individual, individuality and uniqueness, and collectivity and community demonstrate the overall equivalence in the meaning of person in the writing of Walsh and Merton. Merton moves beyond Walsh by taking care to avoid undue abstractness. Person, Merton makes clear, implies immediacy and directness, while nature implies abstraction and knowing the other as object. He places greater emphasis than Walsh on affirming individuality as a possible expression of personhood. Merton is, however, similarly concerned to distinguish personal life with God from self-centered individualism.

We need solitude, Merton insists, lest we become lost in collective thinking and acting. Freedom is likeness to God, according to Merton; it is also the ability to obey God. Development of this freedom is the transcendent direction of personal realization. In addition to this emphasis on freedom in his development of the notion of the person, Merton takes his understanding of person into his description of prayer, which involves an awakening to the level of God's personal love.

In chapter five, person is presented as a unifying key to Merton's writings. To this point, Merton's most developed thought on personhood issues from Merton the spiritual writer. But Merton is also popular as a social critic and commentator on Oriental spirituality. The unity beneath this diversity of interests is to be found in his notion of the person. With regard to social issues, Merton's underlying concern is for the dignity of the human person.

In his dialog with Oriental traditions of spirituality, Merton's point of reference is the person. Merton's person-centered thought is deep enough to allow for the nondual experience of Oriental spirituality; that is where God is experienced as not other.

Chapter five illustrates the value of the insight into the person for understanding Merton and, by implication, the unifying value of this understanding of person for Christian activists in search of theological foundations. Furthermore, this chapter can help Christians who have incorporated elements of Oriental spirituality into their paths. Use of Merton's concept of person can help them to maintain their Christian identity.

The final chapter of this book offers evaluative comments on the meaning of person according to Merton and Walsh. Their insight into the person grounds human identity in God. Such grounding is not habitual in human awareness; thus this element in the thought of Merton and Walsh offers a challenge inherent in the distinction between one's superficial self, or individuality, and one's deeper self, or person. Unfortunately, the Walshian effort to point beyond individuality to personhood involves a denigration of individuality. Merton is more careful to speak of individuality in positive terms. The thought of both, however, is uncompromising in recognizing transcendence as the direction of personal life.

NOTES FOR CHAPTER I

1. Such is the approach and description of person by Beothius, whose sixth-century discussion of the concept of the person is a traditional point of reference for the theological definition of person.
2. William H. Shannon, *Thomas Merton's Dark Path* (New York: Farrar, Straus & Giroux, 1981).
3. For example, see Raymond Bailey, *Thomas Merton on Mysticism* (Garden City: Doubleday, 1975), p. 34; James T. Baker, *Thomas Merton, Social Critic: A Study* (Lexington: University Press of Kentucky, 1971), pp. 11-13; Elena Malits, *The Solitary Explorer* (New York: Harper & Row, 1980), p. 31; Henri Nouwen, *Thomas Merton, Contemplative Critic* (New York: Harper & Row, 1981), p. 27.
4. Richard Cashen, *Solitude in the Thought of Thomas Merton* (Kalamazoo: Cistercian Publications, 1981).
5. Cashen, p. 54. See these influences mentioned on a single page of Merton, in *The Seven Storey Mountain* (New York: New American Library, 1948), p. 216.
6. Shannon, p. 155.
7. Daniel Walsh, "Thomas Merton: The Sense of Mystery," *Saint John's University Off Campus Record*, vol. 9 (summer 1969), p. 160.
8. Walsh, "Theology of Mysticism," group discussion at the Abbey of Gethsemani; Trappist, Kentucky, May 8, 1975; p. 3.
9. Anthony Distefano, "Dan Walsh's Influence on the Spirituality of Thomas Merton," *The Merton Seasonal*, vol. 5 (1980), pp. 4-13; James Finley, *Merton's Palace of Nowhere* (Notre Dame: Ave Maria Press, 1978), p. 156, n. 38.
10. Walsh's unpublished doctoral dissertation is titled "The Metaphysics of Ideas according to Duns Scotus" (Toronto: Medieval Institute, 1933). His most important papers on the notion of the person are unpublished transcriptions of talks titled "Anselm and Duns Scotus on Faith and the Person," a lecture given at the Catholic University of America, 1966, and "Some Intimations of the Person in the Noetic of Knowledge and Love in the Doctrines of St. Thomas and Duns Scotus," a lecture given at St. Meinrad's Abbey, St. Meinrad, Indiana, 1963. (Hereafter this lecture will be cited as "Some Intimations.") The only place where all of Walsh's papers can be found is the Abbey of Gethsemani.
11. John J. Higgins, *Thomas Merton on Prayer* (Garden City: Doubleday, 1975); Anthony Padovano, *The Human Journey* (Garden City: Doubleday, 1982). For bibliographical data on the Bailey, Baker, and Malits works, see note no. 3 above.
12. Alvin W. Hergott, "Thomas Merton and the Image of Man" (M.A. thesis, University of Saskatchewan, 1971), pp. 44-45.
13. Thomas Merton, "The Inner Experience," unpublished manuscript at the Abbey of Gethsemani, Trappist, Kentucky. (Hereafter cited as *IE*.)
14. Edward Rice, *The Man in the Sycamore Tree* (Garden City: Doubleday, 1970), p. 79.

II

THE THEOLOGICAL CONTEXT

TO UNDERSTAND MERTON'S NOTION of the person, more is needed than description in terms of polarity presentation. We can add to our understanding by delimiting Merton's theological context and his anthropology.

The problems involved in trying to determine a context for Merton's thought are his nonsystematic approach and the great number of works from his hand. Though he never claimed to be systematic, perhaps he gives a hint to those who would try to organize his thought in this attempt to summarize the contents of his own work:

> Whatever I may have written, I think it can all be reduced in the end to this one root truth: that God calls human persons to union with Himself and with one another in Christ, in the Church which is His Mystical Body. . . . But if I have written about interracial justice, or thermonuclear weapons, it is because these issues are terribly relevant to one great truth: that man is called to live as a son of God. Man must respond to this call to live in peace with all his brothers in the One Christ.[1]

However accurate this summary may be, it is unsatisfactory to the extent that it focuses exclusively on the goal of human life, for Merton has written on more than the goal. Yes, the call to union is an important part of his writings, and his social comment does relate to union. But what about all of Merton's descriptions of the obstacles to union, of the struggles of Christian and monastic life, of the failure to achieve union that humans experience? To be faithful to Merton's theological anthropology I must write about the negative experiences of life as well as the goal.

In reading Merton's published and unpublished works and allowing themes to emerge, one sees many descriptions of the obstacles to union. Furthermore, one sees references to twelfth-century Cistercian teaching on image of God at all periods of Merton's career as a writer. For example, as early as the late 1940s, in his commentaries on St. Bernard of Clairvaux (1948)[2] and in *The Waters of Siloe* (1949),[3] Merton was looking to twelfth-century Cistercians when expressing his vision of the human being. In these early works, Merton does more than give history lessons when he invokes Bernard of Clairvaux and other Cistercian fathers. He interweaves their thought with his own, moving back and forth with ease. He even uses first-person pronouns, which fact demonstrates that he identifies with Bernard's thought. Examples of this moving about from the twelfth-century to his own experience are abundant. In the following passage, he is discussing true versus false solitude:

> True interior solitude is simply the solitude of pure detachment — a solitude which empties *our* hearts and isolates *us* from the desires and ambitions and conflicts and troubles and lusts common to all the children of this world. And so, in urging his monks to leave the world and all it stands for, St. Bernard insisted they should concentrate on being unlike the common run of men and enter into the loneliness of the saint.[4]

Merton identifies with Cistercian experience even to the point that St. Bernard is addressing him on how he and his twentieth-century brethren are to live. This early identification with Bernard's teaching on the way of Christian life does not leave Merton. In "The Inner Experience," which Merton wrote in the late 1950s, he refers to Bernard's teaching on contemplation;[5] in the early 1960s, in *The New Man*, he writes of Adam's sin and refers to Bernard.[6] These references merely show that Merton continues to invoke as a theological authority the same Bernard of Clairvaux whose teaching he earlier had identified with (as evidenced by those first-person pronouns).

Especially impressive is that Merton, during his last talk before his death, in which he was trying to point out a difference between Christian and Marxist anthropologies, cites twelfth-century Cistercian teaching:

> So our myth of original sin, as explained for example by St. Bernard, comes very close indeed to the Buddhist concept of avidya, of this fundamental ignorance. Consequently, Christianity and Buddhism look primarily to a transformation of man's consciousness — a transformation and a liberation of the truth imprisoned in man by ignorance and error.[7]

Merton is talking about union; but because of sinfulness, the door to union is transformation, and transformation in Bernard's terms. Note how Merton moves from Bernard's teaching to a generalization about Christianity as though for Merton Bernard's teachings are representative of Christian teaching.

Later in that same last talk (pp. 333-334), Merton again invokes twelfth-century Cistercian teaching in order to express the heart of Christian monastic transformation:

> You find, for example, the Cistercians of the 12th century speaking of a kind of monastic therapy. Adam of Perseigne has the idea that you come to the monastery, first, to be cured. . . . When one makes one's profession, one has passed through convalescence and is ready to begin to be educated in a new way — the education of the "new man." The whole purpose of the monastic life is to teach men to live by

love. The simple formula, which was so popular in the West, was the Augustinian formula of the translation of *cupiditas* into *caritas*, of self-centered love into an outgoing, other-centered love. In the process of this change the individual ego was seen to be illusory and dissolved itself, and in place of this self-centered ego came the Christian person, who was no longer just the individual but was Christ dwelling in each one. So in each one of us the Christian person is that which is fully open to all other persons because ultimately all other persons are Christ.

Given Merton's long association with twelfth-century Cistercian teaching on union, sinfulness, and transformation, we may safely look to Bernard's teaching on Christian transformation for ways of organizing Merton's personalistic thought. For Bernard and the twelfth-century Cistercians influenced by him, humans are made in the image of God for union with God, but, because of their sinfulness, they must pass through a period of ascetical reformation. Since Bernard and Merton symbolize union with God by the notion of "the new man," there must also be an "old man."[8] The "old man" symbolizes Adam, whose fallen condition all share.

The drama of union attained through transformation of one's fallen condition originates with God's love. Image-of-God teaching links human life with God from beginning to end. Merton tells the story of human life in terms of origin in God, fall into unlikeness to God, and return to God. This threefold version of the Christian story is more complete than Merton's above-quoted summary, where he is speaking about union. Union implies disunion; more of the story is needed. This three-act version has a beginning, middle, and end and, thus, contextualizes the meaning of person for Merton.

Elena Malits rightly points to Merton's acknowledgment of his own reliance upon Bernard of Clairvaux's teaching on false versus true self, but she does not tell us where in Bernard such teaching occurs.[9] Merton writes in *Waters of Siloe*, around 1948, that in the language of St. Bernard, "our true personality has been concealed under the disguise of a false self, the *ego* whom we tend to worship in place of God."[10] I do not know why Malits does not direct the reader to specific texts in Bernard; one reason may be that, despite Merton's assurance about "Bernard's language," the exact vocabulary of true versus false self does not occur in Bernard. What one finds in Bernard is language of true self[11] and image-of-God concealed.

The clearest examples are in Bernard's *Sermons on the Song of Songs*. In sermons 81 and 82, Bernard speaks of an indestructible and threefold likeness to the Logos: "simplicity of essence," "perpetuity of life," and "free choice."[12] This threefold likeness is covered by deception, pretense, and hypocrisy. (82.2) Bernard speaks of the creature being "covered with confusion as with a cloak." The soul as image of God (82.3, 82.5) is "clothed" and "covered"

> with the folds of likeness and unlikeness. Is deceit not like the folds of a cloak, being not inborn but put on and, so to speak, with the needle of sin stitched on to simplicity, as death is to immortality, and compulsion to freedom? (82.5)

This unlikeness is voluntary, and yet, Bernard says in the same passage, "the primal likeness remains."

To corroborate the hypothesis that Merton's true-versus-false-self language, which he ascribes to Bernard, is actually Merton's own language used to interpret Bernard's teaching in his *Sermons on the Song of Songs*, let us examine Merton's commentary on this sermon of Bernard. There Merton writes that there is always present in fallen man "this persistent tendency to make himself like unto God, to put himself in the place of God, that is, to make his own ego the center of the universe."[13]

Merton goes on, on p. 119, to assert that "on earth our chief, in fact our only task, is to get rid of . . . the overlying layer of duplicity that is not ourselves." He also specifies, on p. 118, that the whole life of the monk "will consist in *being himself*, or rather trying to return to the original simplicity, immortality, and freedom which constitute his real self, in the image of God." Here we see Merton's true-versus-false-self language in embryonic form. He sees the real self as image of God and the lost likeness as a result of the false self. Merton translates Bernard's image-and-likeness teaching into true and false self. In *Thomas Merton on St. Bernard*, Merton comments on the major works of Bernard plus a few lesser sermons. His commentary is designed to explicate the way of monastic living in service of restoration to likeness to God and union with God. The sloughing off of obstacles, or of false self, is the purpose of monastic asceticism. The entire monastic life, Merton, in harmony with Bernard, sees as a school for return to union with the Word.

We will be faithful to Merton's vision of the human person by using the traditional categories of Bernard's vision of Christian life as framework for understanding Merton. Bernard's vision, however, draws much from earlier monasticism and from Augustine.

From Bernard and Augustine (and Plotinus through Augustine), Merton borrows the term "region of unlikeness" to describe the situation of fallenness. In the language of Bernard, self-knowledge includes knowledge of one's own misery; Merton speaks of this knowledge of self as "compunction," or "dread." The emphasis on compunction as part of the way of liberation, or return to God, is traditionally monastic as well as Cistercian.[14]

A final point on which Bernard is helpful for understanding Merton is on the use of *nothing* or *nothingness* when referring to self. Both Bernard and Merton use *nothing* in positive and negative senses, as goal and as problem.

Creation in the Divine Image

MERTON IS IN ACCORD WITH WALSH in teaching that creation emerges from God's creative love. Noting in the manner of Psalm 104 how all creatures praise God, Merton comments: "Their being, their life and their beauty existed because they were known by Him . . . these things praised Him because they were decided in His liberty. . . . Their being was their obedience to His option."[15] The same point can be made here as with Walsh that the divine act of love is at the heart of all being, and the challenge of being human is to discover and consciously live out this loving relationship. The above description of creation occurs in the chapter of *The New Man* called "Image and Likeness," a title that discloses the significance of creation for Merton. The divine and the human meet in knowing and loving.

For Merton, as for Bernard of Clairvaux, image of God is seen through human freedom" (p. 63). "The capacity for freedom and love," writes Merton, "is the image of God because God himself is pure freedom and pure love."[16] Human freedom is a mirror of God's liberty.[17] Although the mirror is "distinct from the image reflected in it,"[18] the human image involves a "participation in the freedom of God"(p. 81). Since God is simple, such participation is also a participation in the being of God (p. 8).

To appreciate Merton's understanding of the relationship between God and human beings, we will profit from Jose Pereira's typology of [1] the difference tradition, which emphasizes the difference between God and creation, especially the human part; [2] the unity tradition, which emphasizes the identity between God and creation; and [3] the unity-in-difference tradition, which emphasizes the unity while maintaining the difference between God and creation.[19]

Merton, unwilling to ignore the distinction between Creator and creature, writes that "there is an infinite metaphysical gulf between the being of God and the being of the soul, between the 'I' of the Almighty and our own inner 'I'"[20] In this distinction, Merton affirms the transcendent otherness of God. But one would err to situate Merton in the difference tradition. He gropes for ways to express the intimacy between God and human beings that ends in a nonobservable touching of what cannot be objectified.

Experientially, Merton is in the unity-in-difference camp, as he says that "God and the soul seem to have but one single 'I'" (p. 12). Here *soul* refers to the true self awakened from its illusory existence; the person, or image of God, never means soul as opposed to body in Merton.[21] In *Zen and the Birds of Appetite*, Merton also asserts unity in difference by saying that "the distinction between creator and creature does not alter the fact that there is also a basic unity *within ourselves* at the summit of our being where we are 'one with God.'"[22]

For Merton, union with God is union with the uncreated Image, Christ.[23] In Christ, the image of God in humans is liberated and is found incorporated into the unity of one "mystical Person."[24] Later the themes of Christ and liberation will be developed further, but the important point here is that the meaning of the human person for Merton is image *of* — that is, a being *in relation to* God, participating in God's own freedom and life. Divine image is Merton's anthropological starting point; later this image will be clarified in light of the fall. The divine image in Merton's anthropological vision is the primal innocence. The innocence regained is the true self liberated from the effects of having fallen into the region of unlikeness. The image of God in human beings is a "dynamic tendency"[25] that leads to union with God. The interference with that dynamic tending makes sin an experience of frustration. According to Merton, we are primarily images of God, but fallen images on a difficult journey to Him.

Region of Unlikeness

BECAUSE HUMAN IMAGING OF GOD is fundamentally determined by a relatedness to Him, as the mirror metaphor suggests, the fallen condition involves a falling away from a human way of relating to God. Some of the patristic and medieval writers distinguish between image and likeness. For Bernard of Clairvaux, the image is the unchanging element where likeness to God can be lost and regained. Merton assumes this language in *The New Man* (p. 125). The traditional description of fallenness employs the metaphor of the region of unlikeness to God. The primal innocence lost in Adam leads to a wandering through a region where the person is enmeshed in ignorance and sin. This metaphor derives from Plato, through Plotinus, to Augustine, then to Bernard of Clairvaux and William of St. Thierry.[26]

Merton occasionally speaks of falling into the "region of

unlikeness,"[27] but his preferred metaphor is the false, illusory, or empirical self. Each of these terms is the negative in a pair: illusory, or false, versus true; empirical versus transcendent; exterior versus interior. Merton gives his most concise statement of the situation of fallenness in "The Inner Experience." There he accepts the teaching on the human image of God that Adam was "created a contemplative."[28]

> Man fell from the unity of contemplative vision into the multiplicity, complication and distraction of an active, worldly existence. Since he was now dependent entirely on exterior and contingent things, he became an exile in a world of objects, each one capable of deluding and enslaving him. Centered no longer in God and in his inmost spiritual self, man now had to *see* and *be aware* of himself, as if he were his own god. He had to study himself as a kind of pseudo-object, from which he was estranged. And to compensate for the labors and frustrations of this enstrangement, he must try to admire, assert and gratify himself at the expense of others like himself. . . . man's mind is enslaved by an inexorable concern with all that is exterior, transient, illusory, and trivial. And carried away by his pursuit of alien shadows and forms, he can no longer see his own true inner "face," or recognize his identity in the spirit and in God, for that entity is secret, invisible, and incommunicable. But man has lost the courage and the faith without which he cannot be content to be "unseen." He is pitifully dependent on self-observation and self-assertion. That is to say, he is utterly exiled from God and from his own true self. . . . He is tempted to seek God, and happiness, outside himself. So his quest for happiness becomes, in fact a flight from God and from himself . . . further and further away from reality. In the end, he had to dwell in the "region of unlikeness," having lost his inner resemblance to God in losing his freedom to enter his own home, which is the sanctuary of God.[29]

This lengthy quotation contains key elements in Merton's description of the fallen condition. The fall is into self-assertion, self-concern, distraction, and worldliness; into exteriority, delusion, and diminishment of freedom.

Exteriority expresses distraction and worldliness and, paradoxically, is linked with a distorted interiority called narcissism, which is the antithesis of the true inner self. The self-concern, or self-preoccupation, to which Merton frequently alludes is the negative pole of self-transcendence, or centering on God. Self-assertion is symptomatic of illusory identity.

Narcissism

TO BE CAUGHT UP in exteriority, or in the "pursuit of alien shadows," is a classical description of the problem of human existence. Augustine writes of being out of touch with God, whose light shines within: "For that light was within and I was out of doors. That was not in space, but my mind was intent on things which were in space, and I could find no place there to rest."[30] To be outside oneself, looking for happiness outside oneself, is a Plotinian as well as Augustinian description of alienation from self. Plotinus writes:

> Let him who can, follow and come within, and leave outside the sight of his eyes and not turn back to the bodily splendours which he was before. When he sees the beauty in bodies he must not run after them; we must know that they are images, traces, shadows, and hurry away to That which they image.[31]

Plotinus, in the same place, refers to the Narcissus myth as a metaphor for this type of alienation:

> For if a man runs to the image and wants to seize it as if it was the reality (like a beautiful reflection playing on the water, which some story . . . said . . . a man wanted to catch and sank down into the stream and disappeared) then let this man who clings to beautiful bodies and will not let them go, will

... in soul, not in body, sink down into the dark depths and stay blind in Hades consorting with shadows. ...

For Plotinus, narcissism means to be seeking images of self rather than of the One. Such narcissism involves a failure to orient self toward the higher reality and a reduction of other realities to one's own selfish level. This failure to look above or within is a function of looking without, or exteriority.

Thanks to the psychoanalytic movement, narcissism is a popular concept, though the transcendent dimension often is not mentioned. Freud gives his own description of narcissism: "In rare cases one can observe that the ego has taken itself as an object and is behaving as though it were in love with itself."[32] Freud's description is useful here because is shows that the problem of narcissism includes dominance of object-centered consciousness. The One, the transcendent Goal, for Plotinus, is not an object. The connection between exteriority and this wrong sort of interiority is the relating to self as object as well as the aforementioned misplacement of one's desire. Thus the parameters of narcissism include an object-centered consciousness and a fascination with one's self.

Merton repeatedly applies the term *narcissism* to false interiority, to ways of turning inwards with the appearance of seeking God but ending with a complacent wallowing in one's inner comfort. The way of prayer is

> not mere negation. Nor can a person become a contemplative merely by "blacking out" sensible realities and remaining alone with himself in darkness.... He is not alone with God, but alone with himself.... He becomes immersed and lost in himself, in a state of inert, primitive and infantile narcissism.[33]

Instead of the journey to God, some seek their own peace apart from God.[34] This "narcissistic peace," as Merton calls it,[35] expresses an unconscious alienation from truth. The way of prayer, according to Merton, should mean a commitment to ongoing conversion, a willingness to be taught and led:

Far from establishing oneself in unassailable narcissistic security, the way of prayer brings us face to face with the sham and indignity of the false self that seeks to live for itself alone and to enjoy the "consolation of prayer" for its own sake.[36] This self uses the relational activity of prayer as a means for its own consolation.

Secularized Existence

THIS SELF-CENTERED EXISTENCE, Merton believes, is the way of worldly life. Merton, as a member of a religious order that practiced "separation from the world" yet in a Church that was turning to the world, naturally wrestled with this question of the world.[37] In "The Inner Experience," he avoids the more ambiguous term *world* for secular-versus-sacred attitude. Etymologically, *secular* derives from *saeculum*, which connotes a temporal dimension to world, since it means century as well as world. "The saeculum," Merton writes, "is that which is temporal, which changes, revives, and returns again to its starting point."[38] The Greek *kuklon*, meaning wheel or cycle, may be underneath the meaning of *secular* as well. Thus as Merton writes in the same place, the secular is "that which goes around in interminably recurring cycles, and a life is

> secularized when it commits itself completely to the "cycles" of what *appears to be new* but is in fact the same thing over again. Secular life is a life of vain hopes, imprisoned in the illusion of newness and change, an illusion which brings us constantly back to the same old point, the contemplation of our own nothingness. Secular life is a life frantically dedicated to escape, through novelty and variety, free from the fear of death.

Secular society escapes through diversion. The escape is from a self that is not grounded in relationship with God.

The secularized person is one who depends upon things to escape from his or her nothingness (p. 38). Here one sees the connection between distractions, worldliness, exteriority, and the distorted interiority of narcissism. All involve escapes from reality, particularly from personal, or relational, reality.

Secular society promotes this escape because secular society cannot make money on deepening one's relationship with God. A monastic society can also fall out of a real relationship with those outside the cloister and thus become "a kind of organized narcissism."[39]

Self-preoccupation

AS FREUD'S UNDERSTANDING of narcissism includes relating to self as object, so too for Merton is this depersonalized mode of relating a part of fallenness. Relating to self as object expresses the self-preoccupation of one whose insecurity has the upper hand.

Without an awareness of being an image of God or being loved by God, one has little more than the reactions of other people as sources of self-worth. Interiority, as well as outreach, becomes relatively ineffectual in communicating God for one whose insecurity is not touched by His love. The inward turn in the name of prayer may fail to lead beyond oneself. The person dominated by insecurity can create a false interiority that searches for ways to prop up an ungrounded self. The self searches for spiritual experiences instead of God in order to reassure this unreal self of its own reality. In this condition, the spiritual aspirant is especially concerned with how he or she is progressing. Unable to trust in God's love, the aspirant seeks signs of being spiritual.[40]

As religious interiority can fail to transcend the self imprisoned by insecurity, so, too, religious activism can mask the lack of awareness of God's affirmation. Instead of reaching out in love, religious activists may flee from their emptiness through the distraction of multiple deeds. Merton cautions James Forest of the Catholic peace movement in a letter to him dated February 21, 1966, against this flight from self:

Do not depend on the hope of results. When you

are doing the sort of work you have taken on, essentially an apostolic work, you may have to face the fact that your work will be apparently worthless and even achieve no result at all, if not perhaps results opposite to what you expect. As you get used to this idea you start more and more to concentrate not on the results but on the value, the rightness, the truth of the work itself. And there too a great deal has to be gone through, as gradually you struggle less and less for an idea and more and more for specific people. The range tends to narrow down, but it gets much more real. In the end, it is the reality of personal relationships that saves everything. . . .

You are probably striving to build yourself an identity in your work, out of your work and your witness. You are using it, so to speak, to protect yourself against nothingness, annihilation. That is not the right use of your work.[41]

The fear of disappearing is a direct consequence of not knowing God's love with sufficient depth.

Both the escape of a false prayer life designed to provide self-assurance and that of religious activism designed to create an identity in one's actions are the helpless flailings of those preoccupied with self. This religious escapism is not as obvious as "secular" diversions.

Self-assertion

ANOTHER WAY MERTON SPEAKS of the situation of fallenness — in addition to exteriority and self-preoccupation — is in terms of self-assertion. Self can don the costume of love in order to attract the attention of others. The "love" offered is a form of "payment with which we buy their recognition of our own existence."[42]

These kinds of "love" or "prayer" or "Christian service" are all forms of self-assertion against the nothingness of selves that are not mirroring God. Such self-assertion is expressed in the New Testament writings as legalism. "The Law offers the self-seeking self the spurious autonomy which comes from creating a place for itself in the minds of men by human righteousness and achievements" (p. 188). The legalism of religious people is far from the only manifestation of self-assertion in the contemporary world. The acquisition of wealth and power is the common path of success. Wealth and power are values that guide autonomous egos. In the presence of God's creation, the law of self-assertion quantifies reality; the beauty of a forest becomes so many thousand board feet. Reality is not seen as it is; rather it is distorted in terms of the competitive values of the self that seeks to establish itself.[43] The self is trapped in this project of self-assertion, but the effort is futile, for the self cannot account for its own existence by itself.

Liberation

THE THIRD ACT IN THE DRAMA of Christian living, according to Merton, is return to God, or liberation. However much Merton advocates human effort, his view of return is Christocentric. Grace-filled human effort to return to God includes faith, self-knowledge, and compunction. Personal relationship with God means growing trust and freedom from efforts to justify self, which Merton treats under the term "uselessness." Finally, return to God is a matter of self-transcendence, both in contemplation and in love of others.

In Christ

RELEASE, OR LIBERATION from the life of futile striving, is a perennial desire of religion. Early in Christian tradition, Paul cries out for salvation: "Who will deliver me from this body of death?" Merton shares his answer: "God, through Jesus Christ."[44] Liberation in Bernard is found in restoration of lost likeness or return to one's sought likeness to Christ, through whom one came into being. Christ is "able to reform what was deformed."[45]

Merton writes of the liberation available in Christ in terms that correspond to his descriptions of fallenness. Liberation will be from exteriority to a self-transcending interiority,[46] self-preoccupation to trust and self-forgetfulness,[47] and from self-assertion to the climate of mercy — that is, to accepting the mercy of God.[48] The situation of fallenness, however described, is symptomatic of ignorance of one's authentic self. One is an image of God, loved by God, yet a creature who is also sinful. The way out of bondage is conversion through awakening to one's true self. This awakening follows the path of self-knowledge and compunction. According to Merton, the possibilities for reorientation and liberation derive from union with Christ.

Merton shows no sign of having been influenced by contemporary Christological debates over the validity of the Council of Chalcedon. The hypostatic union, for Merton, unlocks the greatest possibilities for human beings and reveals "the inner and spiritual significance of man."[49] Chalcedon asserts the divine and human natures of Christ united in one person.

Contemporary critics of this Chalcedonian formulation charge that to say there is no human person in Christ devalues His humanity.[50] Merton, however, sees in the hypostatic union the hope and possibility of divinization. "As a result of this union of God and man in the one Person of Christ it was possible for every man to be united to God in his own person, as a true son of God, not by nature but by adoption."[51] The idea of the lack of a human person in Christ does not strike Merton as dangerous; on the contrary, to be lost in God through union with Him is Merton's goal in life.[52] God became man so that "man might be able to lose himself in man and find himself in God."[53]

The mysteries of the Incarnation and the Crucifixion are proofs of His love as well as patterns for living (pp. 26-27). As patterns, they concretize human possibilities for union with God. In the Incarnation, Merton sees the pattern of self-emptying. As God emptied Himself of His transcendent nobility, so humans should empty themselves of what is ignoble. What Merton means is that humans should divest themselves of their false selves. To give a further Christological anchor to this idea of purification, or sacrifice, Merton notes that in human divinization, all that is truly part of human nature is assumed by Christ; but there should be a "radical cutting off of everything in us that was not assumed by Him because it was not capable of being divinized" (p. 30). In the same place, Merton specifies:

> It is everything that is focused on our exterior and selfish self: everything that can be described as sin, as inordinate or self-centered passion, as self-assertion, greed, lust; as the desire for the survival and perpetuation of our illusory and superficial self, to the detriment of our interior and true self.

This description fits his various descriptions of fallenness as given above. Thus in Christ is the restoration and elevation of fallen human nature to likeness to God.

One may wonder if the Resurrection is a pattern for living also. The Resurrection has a future dimension and, in its futurity, draws people on in hope. Merton acknowledges the possibility of transformation into the likeness of Christ through the Resurrection, in "The Inner Experience" (p. 27). The Resurrection means that in the Resurrected Christ, human nature is divinized, thereby giving the possibility for human beings to appropriate their divinization by following Christ.

Human decision and cooperation with God's transforming influence,[54] however necessary, should not obscure the greater-than-individual parameters of liberation in Christ. The foundation for liberation is God's union with human nature in Christ. Individuals respond personally to Christ, but the full meaning of their personhood is found ecclesially. The renewal of human beings through the establishment of personal love relationships with God occurs "as *Ecclesia* as 'one new man'" (ibid.). To be fully a person means to be incorporated into the one mystical Person of Christ. The intention of Christ, in Merton's words, is that all "might become One Son of God in Christ."[55]

Becoming one with Christ expresses Merton's conviction that the union to which personhood is oriented is greater than the meaning that can be found in an individual, however clarified his or her undividedness may be! The liberation of human beings from their fallenness is preeminently through Christ's hypostatic union, with Christ in the patterns of living He exemplified, and into the personal love of Trinitarian life. With this Christological foundation for liberation set, the human cooperative activities come into view.

Faith

THE RETURN TO GOD, or the restoration of likeness to God, occurs through faith, which includes self-knowledge and compunction as well as self-transcendence through contemplation.

Of the many meanings of faith,[56] three stand out in Merton's writings: trust, illumination, and intellectual assent. Faith experientally connects God and human beings. Part of faith includes intellectual assent; the content of faith includes the Christian story, or Christian revelation.

Intellectual Assent

MERTON STRESSES THAT FAITH is more than intellectual surrender to dogma.[57] The assent to doctrines is a part of Merton's faith that remained orthodox. His is a monastic theology geared to articulate the spiritual journey. He was given scholastic theology in the monastery as part of his priestly formation and never totally repudiated scholasticism. His own monastic vocation, however, would prevent him from disconnecting intellect from life. His intellectual fidelity to Christian and, particularly, Catholic tradition is not symptomatic of an intellectual evasion of the search for God beyond human grasp.

Intellectual assent involves an acknowledgment of mystery and a way of integrating the unknown into one's life.[58] That faith is more than intellectual assent means to Merton that one's commitment to God is made by one's whole self.[59] The intellect, however, is important. Knowing that one is held in being by God[60] is an important experience for Merton, and that knowing includes the intellectual grasp of that idea. Such a grasp, however, will not have a profound effect on one's life unless one's emotions and will center upon that insight. The assent to God through faith is as total a commitment as one can make to another person.

Illumination

FAITH, AS WELL AS INTELLECTUAL ASSENT, is also a way of knowing; this way of knowing is traditionally called illumination. Christian Platonists, including Pseudo-Dionysius and Augustine, use the imagery of light when they speak of knowing. Merton also speaks of illumination by the light of Christ.[61] The technical, Augustinian meaning of illumination through the influence of the Ideas in the mind of God upon one's understanding is not Merton's. He does not reject that explanation of illumination, but he is not concerned to expound epistemological theory. The writings of Merton reveal the illuminating function of faith in the gift of understanding oneself in the light of God.

In "The Inner Experience," Merton writes (on p. 24) that illumination of one's inmost self is the perfection of faith. In *Love and Living*, he speaks of faith "leading to the abandonment of our old understanding of ourselves, of our relationship to God and to the world, and to the discovery of our new identity in Christ."[62] This discovery is a function of faith as illumination. Self-knowledge in Merton does not refer to isolated self but always to self in relation to God. The intellectual assent to dogma passes into illumination as the Christian story becomes one's own story.

The Self as Loved

SELF-KNOWLEDGE IN MERTON, as well as in his Cistercian master, Bernard of Clairvaux, is two-pronged. To know oneself as loved by God, as image of God, is to possess the definitive insight. Bernard speaks of human dignity in terms of its source: "By knowledge I mean that by which [a person] recognizes that his dignity is within himself but not from himself."[63] Ignorance of oneself as gift leads to a straying from truth through curiosity or distraction. The person in ignorance of human dignity fashions self according to sensible creatures. Ignorance of oneself as gift can lead to thinking of oneself as less than one is: as a merely sensory being; or as more than one is: as the source of one's goodness (2.4).

Merton similarly expresses this first prong of self-knowledge as understanding oneself as affirmed by God rather than one's ego-identity trying to establish itself, when he says that

> we fabricate a trifling and impertinent identity for ourselves with the bare scraps of experience that we find lying within immediate reach. . . .
>
> . . . If we take a more living and more Christian perspective we find in ourselves a simple affirmation which is not of ourselves. It simply *is*. In our being there is a primordial *yes* that is not our own; it is not at our own disposal; it is not accessible to our inspection and understanding; we do not even fully experience it as real (except in rare and unique circumstances). And we have to admit that for most people this primordial "yes" is something they never advert to at all. It is in fact absolutely unconscious, totally forgotten.
>
> Basically, however, my being is not an affirmation of a limited self, but the "yes" of Being itself, irrespective of my own choices. Where do "I" come in? Simply in uniting the "yes" of my own freedom with the "yes" of Being that already *is* before I have a chance to choose. . . . There is reality, and there is free consent. There is the actuality of one "yes." In this actuality no question of "adjustment" remains and the ego vanishes.[64]

Thus for Merton, who one is, is determined by God's love, God's affirmation of oneself. That ground of being must be discovered if one is to be one's genuine self rather than an illusory self.

For both Merton and Bernard, knowledge of self without reference to God is ignorance, but all people share in this ignorance. The problem of self-preoccupation finds resolution through growing awareness of self as loved and held in being by God. With God as one's security base, the need to assert oneself out of feelings of insecurity diminishes.

Self as Creaturely and Sinful

THE SECOND PRONG of self-knowledge in Merton and Bernard takes account of human ignorance. To neglect one's relationship with God is to distort one's likeness to God. Awakening to one's unlikeness to God's image is compunction. For Bernard, this knowledge of one's own sinfulness is the first step toward truth, the truth about oneself. The second step toward truth is the truth about one's neighbor. With the experience of one's own misery, one will go out to others in compassion rather than with judgment.[65] This awareness of the need for God in oneself and others leads to greater attentiveness to God. This Bernardine background fits Merton's positive view of compunction. Merton writes that

> The first step in the monk's ascent to God will be to recognize the truth about himself — and face the fact of his own duplicity. That means: *simplicity in the sense of sincerity*, a frank awareness of one's own shortcomings.[66]

Recognizing the truth about oneself and facing one's duplicity involve the self-knowledge that recognizes one's illusory self as illusion, or as *nothing*, and one's true self as hidden in God and hidden to one's self-preoccupation, hence *nothing*. To appreciate further the positive significance of compunction and knowledge of one's illusions and sinfulness, we will profit by examining Merton's paradoxical use of the terms *nothing* and *nothingness* as both problem and goal for human identity.

One finds in Merton the desire to "vanish," to "be nothing":

> To be a priest means, at least in my particular case, to have nothing, desire nothing, and be nothing but belong to Christ. . . .
> That contemplatives have nothing to do with the active ministry contributes more to our utter poverty. . . . It implies the realization that perhaps we have practically nothing to give to souls in the way of preaching and guidance and talent and inspiration. We are ashamed of any active apostolate that might conceivably come from us. And so we vanish into the Mass. . . .[67]

In addition, Merton admires those who can "get lost in the light of eternity."[68] Loss of self is clearly one of Merton's goals. At the same time, he recognizes lack of identity as a serious problem.[69] The problem of not having an identity and the desire for loss of self will make sense in light of Merton's teaching on compunction.

Lack of Identity

A RECURRING THEME IN MERTON is the problem of lack of identity. The problem consists in a person's being a cog in the social machinery, thus diminishing personal freedom and obscuring the person. A social structure can absorb people and make them subservient to itself. In *Conjectures of a Guilty Bystander*, Merton speaks of being without identity, not being a self but simply a social process.[70] Later, in *Love and Living*, Merton speaks of the individual self, however false, becoming lost in the false general self.[71] In "The Inner Experience," Merton notes the loss of self to the manipulations of totalitarian state or class:

> And this is one of the most dangerous features of our modern barbarism: the invasion of the world by a barbarity from within society and within man himself. Or rather, the reduction of man, in technological society, to a level of almost pure alienation in which

he can be brought, at will, anytime, to a kind of political ecstasy, carried away by the hate, the fear and the crude aspirations centered about a leader, a propaganda slogan or a political symbol.[72]

This political ecstasy, Merton observes, substitutes for religious experience in some:

> It is becoming more and more common for the innate aspirations which all men, as images of God, share for the recovery of their inmost self, to be perverted and satisfied by the mere parody of religious mystery, and the evocation of a collective shadow of a "self." . . . It "feels like" spontaneity, and above all there is the meretricious assurance of greatness and infallibility, and the sweet loss of personal responsibility which one enjoys by abandoning himself to a collective mood, no matter how murderous or how vile it may be in itself. (pp. 18-19)

This is an extreme example of the problem of loss of self: an enslavement and a loss of personal responsibility.

Life in technological society includes enormous social pressures to live in particular ways. Merton observes that a person comes to a monastery in order to be true to self "or at least discover whether or not he is anybody at all."[73] The suffocating influence of life in mass society provides motivation to break loose and breathe one's own air, to search for an identity that is not a product of social pressures. This is a problem Merton experienced in his own life and journey to Christ.

In *The Seven Storey Mountain*, Merton admits that he has to some extent been shaped by social and historical forces:

> I saw clearly enough that I was the product of my times, my society and my class. I was something that had been spawned by the selfishness and irresponsibility of the materialistic century in which I lived.[74]

He qualifies this interpretation of the societal impact on his sinfulness with the observation, in the same passage, that cultural forces affected only the surface of his personality. Beneath the "peculiar character of weak and supercilious flippancy proper to this particular century," one finds the same greed, lust, and selfishness operative in all times and places. Thus, sinfulness for Merton was not merely a matter of social pressure, yet he felt that he had been shaped by the materialism of his society.

In *The Sign of Jonas*, Merton speaks of his feeling of being a nonperson. He speaks of thinking "that perhaps I was not even a real person any more," and of having feelings of "nonexistence."[75] Though the words remind one of the problem of lack of identity, the context reveals that Merton's feelings are connected to compunction, which he believes to be an important part of the purification process.

The context is that Merton is feeling humiliated over having asked to be excused from proclaiming the Gospel at Mass. He had suffered through a worry-filled night and had worn himself out. Why the worry? Five months earlier, on a hot and muggy July day, Merton passed out during the reading of the Gospel at high Mass. The recently ordained Merton was undoubtedly embarrassed by this momentary collapse. Months later, in December, worrying about the possibility of fainting again during the community Mass, he allows himself to be excused from proclaiming the Gospel and serving as deacon for the whole week. Monica Furlong judges this behavior neurotic: "Giving in to his neurosis afforded temporary relief but made him feel weak and ashamed."[76] What is the neurotic element, and what is the connection between his feeling humiliated and feeling nonexistent? Merton says that he "felt lonely and small and humiliated — chopping down dead trees with a feeling that perhaps I was not even a real person anymore."[77]

The worry over the possibility of fainting, and allowing himself to ask to be excused from proclaiming the Gospel, are a bit much; and the feeling of nonexistence sounds extreme. Any new priest would feel some embarrassment at not being able to perform such a simple duty for a reason that is not apparent to anyone else. But the experience of embarrassment need not be linked to "nonexistence," as in this incident.

Merton gives a clue to further interpretation to his feelings of fear and dejection and nonexistence by remarking that it gave him "a kind of satisfaction to realize that it is not by contact with any other creature that I can recover the sense that I am real" (ibid.).

Here Merton acknowledges that his feeling humiliated relates to his identity. To be embarrassed in this way involves feeling that one is dropping out of existence. In the above quote, Merton reflects on the real situation in light of his experience. The real situation is that his sense of his own reality does not depend on the esteem or approval of others.

Merton's reflection that contact with creatures will not enable him to recover his sense of being real expresses his conversion to God and to growth in truth. He responds to this embarrassment by reflecting on his need to grow out of this dependence upon the approval of others for a sense of identity. "Solitude," says Merton in the same place, "means being lonely not in a way that pleases you but in a way that frightens and empties you to the extent that it means being exiled even from yourself."

This final recorded reflection about his embarrassing experience and about feeling nonexistent speaks of the monastic discipline of solitude that leads to a transformation of one's identity. What occurs in solitude is that a person grows in awareness of his or her own falseness and of the need for transformation. This awareness of need for conversion is called compunction.

Compunction and Dread

THE TERM COMPUNCTION ENCOMPASSES Merton's understanding of remorse and dread. Merton distinguishes remorse from dread by saying that the former is "centered on something definite."[78] Remorse is sorrow for having done wrong. Dread is Merton's term for the insecurity and uneasiness of a creature with creaturely faults.[79] Remorse and dread describe feelings of unease that are part of a life of prayer. I use the word *compunction* to apply to the complex of feelings that neither *remorse* nor *dread* exhausts, and because *compunction* is the traditional term that Merton uses to identify one of the acknowledged components of the climate of prayer. He sees the Rule of St. Benedict as trying to create a climate of prayer that consists of "compunction and love."[80]

True compunction is not a symptom of a tyrannical superego.[81] The sense of sin, according to Merton, is not a sense of guilt derived from the violation of the edicts of an authority. Such a feeling of guilt is an oppressive force coming from outside oneself. True compunction "is a sense of evil in myself, not because I have violated a law outside myself, but because I have violated the inmost laws of my own being which are, at the same time, the laws of God who dwells within me."[82]

Thus compunction involves a sense of having thwarted the realization of one's deepest self, or the call of God. Here compunction is symptomatic of one's unlikeness to God. "The sense of sin is the sense of having been deeply and deliberately false to my own inmost reality, my likeness to God" (ibid.). The point Merton stresses in the distinction between superego guilt and true compunction is that the former is a feeling derived from relating to external moral norms, while the latter is an immediate experience of one's falsity to self.

What the concept "dread" highlights in compunction is not sorrow but rather the insecurity of a contingent being. "Dread" says Merton, "is an expression of our insecurity in this earthly life, a realization that we are never and can never be completely 'sure' in the sense of possessing a definitive and established status."[83]

Is dread an expression of contingency or of sinfulness? Such a question would look for human existents not affected by sinfulness. But no such human beings exist. More pertinent to understanding dread is the insight that the insecurity of contingency, the lack "of possessing a definitive and established status," is not easily accepted. Nonacceptance of one's contingency is tantamount to the sin of Adam. Thus the insecurity of creatures who have the freedom to resist acceptance of reality is sin, and this kind of sin is part of the experience of all of Merton's readers.

As for "possessing a definitive and established status," there is a status appropriate to creatures — dependence upon God. The "possessing" of this status is clearly not a matter of absolute autonomy but, rather, of the status of image. The image has no reality, no status apart from the prototype. In ignorance of person as image of God, human beings try to exist in a vacuum without reference to origin or end. "I cannot discover my 'meaning,'" Merton says, "if I try to evade the dread which comes from first experiencing my meaninglessness."[84] This discovered meaning of self emerges from relatedness to God.

Without acknowledged connection to one's origin and end, one's being is unaccountable; such a groundless existence is nothing. Here Merton's use of *nothing* and *nothingness* to refer to a problem rather than a goal comes into focus again. Merton describes a person who is overly concerned with self because he is not relating to God:

> His life is "nothing," not in the *dynamic*, mysterious sense in which the "nothing," *nada*, of the mystic is paradoxically also the all, *todo*, of God. It is purely the nothingness of a finite being left to himself and absorbed in his own triviality.[85]

This is the nothingness of the false identity founded upon emptiness. It is a "makeshift identity," which is ontologically nothing.[86] This nothingness without God is equivalent to what Bernard refers to by his use of *nothing*[87] in several places in his *Sermons on the Song of Songs* where he writes, "Without [God] all are nothing."[88]

Examination of the benefits of compunction will help to show how nothingness is not only a problem but also a goal.

Technological society substitutes individuals for persons. Merton believes that the statistical approach to human beings gives a quantitative view of humanity. Such a view makes "the mass of men simply a total of individual units."[89] To view humanity merely as individual units is to overlook the relational dimension, which is the dimension of the person. Merton here sees this oversight as reducing a person to an individual, and an isolated individual is "nothing."

To break from this view, the monk leaves ordinary society, for

> society, itself, institutional life, organization, the "approved way," may in fact be encouraging us in falsity and illusion. The deep root of monastic "dread" is the inner conflict which makes us guess that in order to be true to God and to ourselves we must break with the familiar, established and secure norms and go off into the unknown.[90]

Such a break with secure norms is not identical with entrance into monastic life, which has its own established conventions. This awesome break with society exposes the element of fear in dread, yet one who is willing to go through dread must see in it something salutary.

The most fundamental benefit of compunction is the clarification of one's need for God. Compunction is part of the conversion process, that is, part of the turn toward God, part of the transformation into His likeness. Compunction is a dissatisfaction with self that discloses one's inability to effect this transformation through personal effort. To recognize "that one is living a lie" will help a person to turn toward truth. To recognize one's helplessness, frustration, confusion, ignorance[91] brings a distress that means that one's hope in oneself has been in vain. One has failed to find one's way. The dormant gift of faith blossoms into a recognition of a total need for God. Merton designates compunction, or sense of sin, as the "first step toward spiritual liberation."[92] What he means is that compunction illuminates the obstacle to transformation; the recognized obstacle, sin, points to the need for God as savior (ibid.).

Though compunction is a first step,[93] it is not an experience that should be discarded. As long as there is attachment to one's illusory self, compunction is likely to return with purifying results.[94] Suppose, for example, that a person has turned to God in a life of faith. This person is in danger of regarding conversion as a past event rather than an ongoing process. He or she may cultivate a life of prayer and come to delight in contemplative repose. The recognition of one's freedom from gross vices may lead to complacency. Knowledge of theology and of spiritual life may engender smugness about oneself. Compunction for such a person may be a great blessing because the function of dread is precisely

> to break down this glass house of false interiority and to deliver man from it. It is dread, and dread alone, that delivers a man out of this private sanctuary in which his solitude becomes horrible to himself without God.[95]

In short, dread, or compunction, can move one out of a spiritual illusion. Dread motivates by revealing one's ugliness and falseness. To be locked up with such decay is to be stimulated to desire fresh air. What spiritual complacency means is that one has created an identity out of one's spiritual practices (ibid.). Such a false identity becomes disgusting to the person graced by compunction.

Compunction implies the ability to accept parts of oneself that one had previously rejected or denied. This acceptance is humility, acceptance of the truth about oneself, in Bernard's language. This integration of the darker aspects of self means expansion of one's reality as relational being. This expansion occurs because, as Merton observes, "both our sinfulness and our interiority tend to be rejected in one and the same movement by the exterior self."[96] Fear of discovering what is unflattering can prevent one from coming into greater possession of one's interiority. But acceptance of one's interior confusion, insecurity, and sinfulness does not imply that one is magically washed clean.

Compunction as integration of the rejected parts of oneself can bring new perspective, a perspective that lowers defenses. As long as one is trying to protect oneself from truth, one is living defensively. One is motivated by fear, since the next moment may bring an insight that will threaten the identity of the ego that has carved out an existence in which self is center of the universe. The repentant heart is willing to be led by truth because defensive egoism has not proven to be an adequate response to life. In Merton's view, "The only full and authentic purification is that which turns a man completely inside out, so that he no longer has a self to defend, no longer an intimate heritage to protect against imagined inroads."[97] The inflated ego shrivels, and one is left with nothing to point to in oneself that deserves anything. This descent into nothingness would be intolerable without faith in God's mercy. Merton says that the

> sacred attitude toward life is in no sense an escape from the sense of nothingness that assails us when we are left alone with ourselves. On the contrary it penetrates into that darkness and that nothingness, realizing that the mercy of God has transformed our nothingness into His temple and believing that in our darkness His light has hidden itself.[98]

Contrary to contemporary culture, which advocates diversion to chase away unpleasant feelings, the entrance into one's nothingness is the recognition that only by allowing the illusory self to deflate can one enter the relationship that He has established. The change of perspective that allows a person to see nothingness as God's dwelling place requires more than insight; it is the fruit of "sorrow pouring itself out in *love* and *trust*." (ibid.)

Nothingness as Goal

HERE THE NOTION OF NOTHINGNESS comes full circle from being a problem — that is, not having an identity or being driven by collective ideas — to becoming a meeting ground for God, the desired Goal. Merton says that "Only when we have descended in dread to the center of our own nothingness, by his grace and his guidance, can we be led by him, in his own time, to find him in losing ourselves."[99] Nothingness is a problem for one whose identity is not rooted in God's love. To flee one's dependence upon God is to try to create an identity apart from Him. Nothingness becomes a desired goal for those who understand that the illusory self is an obstacle to becoming lost in God.

Though the language of nothingness is easily associated with Buddhism, John of the Cross, and Eckhart, one finds Bernard of Clairvaux writing of the goal of vanishing and becoming nothing in terms similar to Merton: "To lose yourself, as if you no longer existed, to cease completely to experience yourself, to reduce yourself to nothing is not a human sentiment but a divine experience."[100]

Merton's most positive statement about human nothingness highlights it as a gate to, or potency for, God: "The nothingness within us — which is at the same time the place wherever freedom springs into being — is secretly filled with the presence and light of God as long as our eyes are not on ourselves."[101]

This nothingness as origin of human freedom is the loss of false self as center and acceptance of God as one's ground. Merton poetically expresses this image of a negation as source of life: "Desert and void. The Uncreated is waste and emptiness to the creature. Not even sand. Not even stone. Not even darkness and night. A burning wilderness would at least be something."[102]

Merton here speaks of the nothingness in experiencing God. One may manage to create an identity as advanced spiritual aspirant from the traditional experiences of "darkness and night." Such experience is at least something from which the ego may derive self-satisfaction, but God does not intend to inflate false identities. "But the Uncreated," Merton continues, "is no something. Waste. Emptiness. Total poverty of the Creator: yet from this poverty springs *everything*. The waste is inexhaustible. Infinite Zero. Everything comes from this desert Nothing" (ibid.).

Here the "Nothing" from which everything comes is capitalized, the divine equivalent to human nothingness as goal. The divine and human meet in an ungraspable, unmanipulable, and unobservable mystery.

The problem of human nothingness without God, of not having an identity as image or of having a false identity, is paradoxically resolved in the unobservable meeting of God and the human in Nothing. The way beyond self-seeking and self-concern is through self-knowledge, compunction, dread. "If you are content to be lost," Merton tells us, "you will be found without knowing it, precisely because you are lost, for you are, at last nowhere" (ibid.). To have the courage to let go of an identity rooted in approval by others and self-assertion implies faith in the One whose love holds all things in being.

Compunction is an illumination that exposes one's falsity, clarifies one's need for God, deflates one's ego with its self-assertiveness, and leads one to depend more earnestly upon God.

The question of self-concern arises. Is not compunction, or self-knowledge, another form of self-preoccupation? The experience of dread, in Merton's opinion, drives a person toward God and others but without fleeing from one's interior reality. By self-knowledge, Merton does not indicate endless self-analysis. A danger of the pragmatic mind would be to depend upon self-analysis as a way to make progress.[103] The illuminating grace of compunction is gift, not technique. Self-analysis has value but only insofar as it leads to a greater reliance upon God's mercy.

Trust

THE FRUIT OF SELF-KNOWLEDGE is greater trust in God. The first prong of self-knowledge, that God holds one in being, diminishes the self-concern that arises from insecurity. The other prong, compunction, strips one of the temptation to rely on oneself apart from God. Thus both prongs conspire to eviscerate trust in isolated self-will and the type of self-assertion that expresses ignorance of God as source. Merton writes that

> when man thinks himself powerful, then at every moment he is in desperate need: he is in need of knowledge, strength, control, and he depends on countless instruments. But when man remembers the unfailing power of God, and realizes that because he is the son of God, this power *already belongs to him*, then he does not have to think any more about the things he needs. For what he needs will be given him when he needs it, and in this sense, God will think and act for him. (p. 80)

Merton applies this reflection about trust versus self-assertion to social problems. The social evils of war and poverty are, he says, "the direct result of man's efforts to be his own Providence" (ibid.). Without God's affirmation, isolated self-assertion is at the expense of others.

Uselessness

THE WILLINGNESS TO TRUST GOD may diminish the need to assert oneself. Merton thus introduces the theme of uselessness to the scheme of Christian virtues. As Paul insisted, salvation is a gift that cannot be earned. For Merton, the contemplative life witnesses to trusting in God's saving love. The value of human life is not reducible to productivity:

> We [contemplatives] are called to prefer the apparent uselessness, the apparent unproductiveness, the apparent inactivity of simply sitting at the feet of Jesus and listening to him. We are called to prefer this over an apparently more productive, more active, more busy life. We quietly affirm that there is something more important than "getting things done."[104]

Here uselessness expresses freedom from self-justification. Although Merton's reflections are concerned with the contemplative versus the active vocation, his linking of uselessness to attentiveness to Jesus makes "uselessness" valuable to any Christian:

> In the active life love is channeled into something that gets results. In the so-called contemplative life love is sufficient unto itself. It does of course work, it does do things, but in our life the emphasis is on love above everthing else, on faith above everything else. Especially on faith above works! The characteristic of our life is that it makes us realize more deeply how much we depend directly on God by faith, how much we depend directly on the mercy of God, how much we depend upon receiving everything directly from him and not through the mediation of our own activity. (p. 386)

Uselessness, in Merton's language, is not only freedom from self-justification but also freedom from the dehumanizing pressure to conform, a freedom from trying to measure up to human standards (ibid.).

The meaning of personhood lies in relatedness to God, not in relatedness to the mass mind that defines human worth in terms of productivity or to one's own insecurity, which seeks reassurance through success. That love of God is sufficient source of meaning and motivation. In Merton's view, monastic life, because of its uselessness, is a defenseless witness to God's love.[105] Consider the mass of humanity, frantically and anxiously trying to attract love and approval. Awakening to God's unconditional love will mean a growing freedom from that anxiety as well as growth in trust.

Contemplation

CONTEMPLATION, MERTON TEACHES in "The Inner Experience," is the full blossoming of trust and illumination of one's personhood in God:

> There is no strain in real contemplation because when the gift is real, you do not depend on it, you are not enslaved by the "need" to experience anything. The contemplative does not seek reassurance in himself, in his virtue, in his state, in his "prayer." His trust is in God, not in himself. The peace and "rest" of contemplation are the fruit of a living faith in the action of divine grace. The contemplative is able to let go of himself and everything else, knowing that everything that matters in his life is in God's hands, and that he does not have to "take thought for the morrow." He fully realizes the meaning of the Gospel message of salvation by the grace of God and not by dependence on human ingenuity.[106]

The rest associated with contemplation is a byproduct of trust and illumination; such rest could become an idol if sought for its own sake. Merton gives an image of genuine contemplative liberation in an early poem, "A Psalm," first published in 1949:

> When psalms surprise me with their music
> And antiphons turn to rum
> The Spirit sings: the bottom drops out of my soul
> And from the center of my cellar, Love, louder
>   than thunder,
> Opens a heaven of naked air.[107]

The setting is the monastic choir. The bottom dropping out in contact with God's love is a picture of the felt relaxation of one's tight ego control over oneself.[108] To use another metaphor of contemplation: if one is held, one need not hold on for dear life.[109] Rest and the bottom's dropping out and being held are all metaphors for contemplative experience as self-transcendence.

Where Merton tries to describe contemplative prayer, he generally includes lengthy qualifications. Such qualifications should caution against indulging in much description of contemplative experience. For example, in *Contemplative Prayer*, Merton notes the ambiguity of the word *contemplation*, which may connote an elitism that would amount to an escape from the ordinary Christian economy of salvation.[110]

In *Zen and the Birds of Appetite* and in *New Seeds of Contemplation*, Merton carefully describes what contemplation is *not*. In *Zen and the Birds of Appetite*, what contemplation is not precedes discussion of the subject of transcendent experience. That order of presentation points to the heart of the problem of trying to discuss contemplation. Such discussion easily feeds the needy ego with feelings of self-importance.[111] The most pointed of Merton's qualifications about describing contemplation appears in *New Seeds of Contemplation*, in which he devotes an entire chapter to what contemplation is not. He says, "The only way to get rid of misconceptions about contemplation is to experience it."[112]

To embark upon a psychological description of contemplation, according to Merton, is to miss the mark (ibid.). Contemplation is not something that one can isolate from a loving relationship with God. In other words, contemplation is intrinsically self-transcendent and cannot be reduced to something the self contains. Merton proceeds, in *New Seeds*, to try to clarify contemplative experience by negating opportunities for the superficial self to acquire status and by pointing in the direction of the person:

> In contemplation abstract notions of the divine essence no longer play an important part since they are replaced by a concrete intuition based on love, of God as a Person, an object of love, not a "nature" or a "thing" which would be the object of study or of possessive desire. (p. 13)

Merton's cautions against trying to define contemplation emerge from his awareness of the situation of fallenness: of self-assertion and self-preoccupation. If the way of liberation is through contemplation as self-transcending, then the central focus of the contemplative must not be his or her own experience but rather God, who is transcendent. Furthermore, if the focus upon God is to be liberating, then God as concept will be replaced by God as Person. To encounter the living God in contemplation means to awaken to His love. Removal of the *what* from religious experience, for Merton as for Walsh, is in service of a *who*. Love is the way of transcendence and liberation.

Love of Others

MERTON'S EMPHASIS ON SOLITUDE somewhat overshadows the theme of the love of other people, but such love is an important element in his treatment of self-transcendence. Merton went to great lengths to place himself in an environment of solitude. At Gethsemani, his yearning for even greater solitude led him to reside in the hermitage on the abbey grounds. Finally, as he traveled to Asia, he was planning to explore other, even more remote sites for his hermitage, which would allow for more continuous exposure to the solitary experience of God. Despite Merton's huge investment in solitude, he affirms that

love for neighbor is a necessary component of self-realization as well as a part of self-transcendence.
Isolation is antithetical to Merton's person-centered thought, even though he speaks of an inner journey. The inward turn of contemplative monastic life carries with it the danger of becoming mired in a swampy introversion that does not attain to self-transcendence. Those who have withdrawn into solitude may fear that interaction with others will diminish the intensity of their inner experience. Merton warns against such self-isolation in terms of burying one's talent; interaction with others expands the heart:

> Even when we come to live a contemplative life, the love of others and openness to others remain, as in the active life, the condition for a living and fruitful inner life of thought and love. The love of others is a stimulus to interior life, not a danger to it, as some mistakenly believe.[113]

The fear that some have of loving others arises from an overvaluation of the monastic value of fleeing distraction.

Related is the fear of friendship. Merton does not write very much about friendship, but what he does write is positive. For example, in a preface to Hallier's *The Monastic Theology of Aelred of Rievaulx*, Merton links friendship with the image of God. "The natural basis for this theology of friendship," he writes, "is of course the indestructible inclination to love, which is the divine image in us."[114] Prior to Vatican II, Aelred of Rievaulx's work *On Spiritual Frienship* had been under lock and key at Gethsemani for years. Thus, although Aelred, a Cistercian, affirmed the value of friendship as part of monastic life, the American Cistercians in Merton's monastery allowed the fear of friendship to restrict circulation of Aelred's teaching.

In this climate, Merton's relative silence about friendship should caution anyone who expects to find in his works a well-developed theology of friendship. He remained primarily committed to the solitary expression of Christian life. Of concern to monastics were "particular friendships." *Particular friendship* at its extreme meant homosexuality. More usually, it meant the absorbing of the attention of two monks in such a way that they lost some of their freedom to be in solitary prayer. In concrete above the guesthouse at Gethsemani are the words GOD ALONE. That motto should be inscribed above this page as well, lest Merton's positive statements about love of others be taken out of context.

In *Contemplation in a World of Action*, Merton tries to correct the misuse of solitude that distorts human affectivity. There he stresses that a mature identity is formed in relation to others: "We discover our identity when we accept our place and our way in the midst of persons and things, in a historical situation. . . ."[115] Similarly, in "The Inner Experience," Merton acknowledges that no one "could arrive at a genuine self-realization unless he had first become aware of himself as a member of a group."[116] Lest the reader forget Merton's monastic context, he notes that an obstacle to self-realization is a "vapid 'togetherness.'"[117]

The way around a superficial togetherness and toward genuine community is in the Person.

> The Christian . . . is One with all his "brothers in Christ." His inner self is, in fact, inseparable from Christ and hence it is in a mysterious and unique way inseparable from all the other I's who live in Christ, so that they all form one "mystical Person," which is "Christ."[118]

The life of God effects self-transcendence by lifting one "above flesh and blood,"[119] that is, above instinctual preferences for one personality over another. The life of God, he writes in the same passage, is activated in loving others:

> In a word, the awakening of the inner self is purely the work of love, and there can be no love where there is not "another" to love. Furthermore one does not awaken his inmost "I" merely by loving God alone, but by loving other men.

This statement suggests that the way of self-transcendence

necessarily includes loving others. The elevation "above flesh and blood" is equivalent to saying "through and beyond the individual to the person." Such transcendence means a new way of relating to others based on the way one relates to oneself. Accepting one's inner self enables a person to see beyond the sinfulness of others. Those who accept themselves "see below the surface to guess at the presence of the inner and innocent self that is the image of God" (p. 40).

Seeing "below the surface" or "above flesh and blood" does not mean blindness toward the individuality of other people. In *Disputed Questions*, Merton condemns the approach to loving Christ in one's neighbor that involves trying to do away with the particularity of that neighbor's personality in order to substitute "a vague and abstract presence of Christ."[120] That form of mental blindness, he says, amounts to loving Christ *instead of* one's neighbor. The point is that relating to other people in the love of Christ means transcending one's comfort-seeking self, which seeks to rest with those whose personalities bring consolation and fails to love those whose character traits do not mesh with one's own. The self-transcendence in Merton's version of the Christian story includes a vision of others as participating in the same personal reality that grounds all of reality.

NOTES FOR CHAPTER II

1. Thomas Merton, "Concerning the Collection in Bellarmine College Library," in The Thomas Merton Studies Center (Santa Barbara: Unicorn Press, 1971), pp. 3-4; quoted in Higgins, p. 14.
2. Merton, *Thomas Merton on St. Bernard* (Kalamazoo: Cistercian Publications, 1980).
3. Merton, *The Waters of Siloe* (New York: Harcourt Brace Jovanovich, 1979), especially the chapter *"Paradisus Claustralis,"* pp. 332-351. Hereafter this book is cited as *WS*.
4. Ibid., p. 345; emphases added.
5. *IE*, appendix, pp. 72, 82, and 83.
6. Merton, *The New Man* (New York: Farrar, Straus & Giroux, 1961), pp. 104-108. Hereafter cited as *NM*.
7. Merton, *The Asian Journal of Thomas Merton* (New York: New Directions, 1975), pp. 332-333. Hereafter cited as *AJ*.
8. In 1948, Merton described Bernard's teaching this way: "St. Bernard's ontology of transforming union is simply an elaboration of a symbol from St. Paul — a symbol which has also become fundamental to the monastic life: the change of garments, the putting off of the old man and the putting on of the new...." *Thomas Merton on St. Bernard*, p. 174; of course, Merton went on to title one of his books *The New Man*.
9. Malits, *Solitary Explorer*, p. 128.
10. *WS*, p. 349.
11. Bernard of Clairvaux, *On the Song of Songs III* (Kalamazoo: Cistercian Publications, 1979), 50.6.
12. Bernard of Clairvaux, *On the Song of Songs IV* (Kalamazoo: Cistercian Publications, 1980), 81.56.
13. *Thomas Merton on St. Bernard*, p. 113.
14. Irenee Hausherr, *Penthos — la doctrine de la componction dans l'Orient Chrétien*, Orientalia Analecta, No. 132 (Rome: Pontifical Oriental Institute, 1944); Jean Leclercq, *Love of Learning and the Desire for God* (New York: Fordham University Press, 1961), pp. 37-41.
15. *NM*, pp. 51-52.
16. Merton, in introduction to *The Monastic Theology of Aelred of Rievaulx* (Spencer, Mass.: Cistercian Publications, 1969), p. ix.
17. *NM*, p. 54.
18. *IE*, p. 8.
19. Jose Pereira, *Hindu Theology* (New York: Image Books, 1976), pp. 37-40.
20. *IE*, p. 8.

21. *NM*, p. 64; see also *IE*, pp. 28-29; Merton, *Contemplation in a World of Action* (New York: Image Books, 1973), p. 201. Hereafter cited as *CWA*.
22. Merton, *Zen and the Birds of Appetite* (New York: New Directions, 1968), pp. 11-12. Hereafter cited as *ZBA*.
23. *NM*, p. 167.
24. *IE*, p. 15.
25. *NM*, p. 121.
26. For a discussion of this region of unlikeness, see Etienne Gilson, *"Regio dissimilitudinis de Platon à Saint Bernard de Clairvaux," Medieval Studies*, vol. 9: pp. 108-130. For key texts see Plato, *Statesman*, 273 d; *Theatetus*, 176 a, b; Plotinus, *Enneads* 1.8.13; Augustine, *Confessions*, 7; Bernard of Clairvaux, *On Grace and Free Will*, 10.32; *On the Song of Songs*, 36.5; *Letters*, 8.2; William of St. Thierry, *Exposition on the Song of Songs*, 1.65; *Meditations*, 4.6.
27. *IE*, pp. 12, 25; *New Seeds of Contemplation* (New York: New Directions, 1961), p. 280, hereafter cited as *NS*.
28. In *NM*, pp. 59-60, Merton holds out this line of thought as one option next to Adam as co-creator.
29. *IE*, pp. 25-26.
30. Augustine, *Confessions*, 7.7.
31. Plotinus, *Enneads*, 1.6.7-8; English translation by A.H. Armstrong; *Plotinus* (London: Allen and Unwin, 1953), pp. 136-137.
32. Sigmund Freud, *New Introductory Lectures on Psychoanalysis* (New York: W.W. Norton, 1964), p. 102; see also Erich Fromm, *The Art of Loving* (New York: Harper & Row, 1956), p. 118, for a related understanding of narcissism.
33. Merton, *The Climate of Monastic Prayer* (Kalamazoo: Cistercian Publications, 1969), p. 123, hereafter cited as *CMP*; reprinted as *Contemplative Prayer* (Garden City: Image Books, 1971), p. 90, hereafter cited as *CP*.
34. Merton also writes of distortion of love as narcissistic, in *Love and Living* (New York: Bantam Books, 1980), p. 32, hereafter cited as *LL*; reprinted by Farrar, Straus, & Giroux.
35. *CWA*, p. 63.
36. *CMP*, p. 36; reprinted as *CP*, p. 24.
37. *CWA*, pp. 159-172; *LL*, pp. 106-110.
38. *IE*, p. 37.
39. *CWA*, p. 233.
40. *CMP*, pp. 53, 57, 145; reprinted as *CP*, pp. 37, 40, 108.
41. Merton, quoted in James H. Forest, "Merton's Peacemaking," *Sojourners* (December 1978), p. 18.
42. *LL*, p. 184.

43. Ibid., p. 195; *IE*, p. 13.
44. Romans 7:24-25.
45. Bernard of Clairvaux, *On Grace and Free Choice* (Kalamazoo: Cistercian Publications, 1977), 10.32, 33.
46. *CMP*, p. 128; reprinted as *CP*, p. 94; *IE*, p. 30.
47. *IE*, p. 50.
48. See *LL*, pp. 184-185.
49. *IE*, p. 28.
50. For an overview of some criticial issues associated with Chalcedon, see G. O'Collins, *What Are They Saying about Jesus?* (New York: Paulist, 1977), pp. 1-12.
51. *IE*, p. 28.
52. Merton. *The Sign of Jonas* (New York: Harcourt Brace Jovanovich, 1979), p. 191; *CMP*, p. 137; reprinted as *CP*, p. 101. Hereafter cited as *SJ*.
53. *IE*, p. 26.
54. See *LL*, p. 203.
55. *IE*, p. 28.
56. Avery Dulles, *The Survival of Dogma* (Garden City: Doubleday, 1971), pp. 15-25.
57. See *LL*, p. 206; *IE*, pp. 10, 32.
58. See *NS*, pp. 137-138.
59. *IE*, p. 32.
60. *NS*, p. 37.
61. *IE*, p. 10.
62. *LL*, p. 206.
63. Bernard of Clairvaux, *On the Love of God*, trans. by Terrence L. Connolly (New York: Spiritual Book Associates, 1937), 1.2.
64. Merton, *Conjectures of a Guilty Bystander* (New York: Doubleday, 1968), pp. 265-266. Hereafter, *CGB*.
65. Bernard of Clairvaux, *On the Steps of Humility*, 3.6.
66. *Thomas Merton on St. Bernard*, p. 119.
67. *SJ*, p. 191.
68. *CWA*, pp. 227-228.
69. For example, *LL*, pp. 16, 51; *IE*, pp. 18-19; *CGB*, pp. 108-109.
70. *CGB*, pp. 108-109.
71. *LL*, p. 51.

72. *IE*, p. 18.
73. *CWA*, p. 71; see also p. 57.
74. *SSM*, p. 135.
75. *SJ*, p. 249.
76. Monica Furlong, *Merton: A Biography* (New York: Bantam Books, 1980), p. 176.
77. *SJ*, p. 249.
78. *CMP*, p. 133; reprinted as *CP*, p. 98.
79. *CMP*, pp. 36, 131; reprinted as *CP*, pp. 24, 97.
80. *CMP*, p. 48; reprinted as *CP*, p. 33.
81. John W. Glaser, "Conscience and Superego," *Theological Studies*, no. 32 (March 1971), pp. 30-47.
82. *IE*, pp. 53-54.
83. *CMP*, p. 138; reprinted as *CP*, p. 101.
84. *CMP*, p. 94; reprinted as *CP*, p. 68.
85. *CMP*, p. 123; reprinted as *CP*, p. 90.
86. *CGB*, p. 224.
87. John F. Teahan, in his "A Dark and Empty Way: Thomas Merton, the Apophatic Tradition," *Journal of Religion*, no. 58 (July 1978), pp. 263-287, links Merton's use of negative language with the influence of John of the Cross. I do not deny that influence but desire to show that Bernard's negative language, which is not generally appreciated, supports Merton's use of *nothingness*.
88. Bernard of Clairvaux, *On the Song of Songs*, 4.4; see also sermon 50.6, 7.
89. *LL*, p. 16.
90. *CMP*, p. 36; reprinted as *CP*, p. 24.
91. *CMP*, p. 50; reprinted as *CP*, pp. 34-35.
92. *IE*, p. 53.
93. Merton, *Seasons of Celebration* (New York: Farrar, Straus & Giroux, 1964), p. 70.
94. *CMP*, p. 138; reprinted as *CP*, p. 102; *IE*, p. 39.
95. *CMP*, pp. 145-146; reprinted as *CP*, p. 108.
96. *IE*, p. 40.
97. *CMP*, p. 147; reprinted as *CP*, p. 109.
98. *IE*, p. 39.
99. *CMP*, p. 137; reprinted as *CP*, p. 101.

100. Bernard of Clairvaux, *Treatises II: On Loving God*, trans. Robert Walton (Washington: Cistercian Publications, 1971), 10.27.
101. *IE*, p. 49.
102. *The Collected Poems of Thomas Merton* (New York: New Directions, 1980), p. 452.
103. *IE*, p. 62. Here Merton writes with irony: "The average man of our time is disposed to be a contemplative in reverse, a mystic of technocracy or of business. His contemplation will be a pragmatic affair, something eminently worthwhile which, if you go about it by the approved and latest methods, will bring quick results. And here psychological self-analysis comes in: indeed, maybe a battery of tests will help you find out whether or not you have a contemplative vocation. In any case, you have to watch yourself and your complexes."
104. *CWA*, p. 374; see also p. 49.
105. See *CWA*, pp. 27, 240, 374.
106. *IE*, p. 50.
107. Merton, *Collected Poems*, p. 220.
108. Merton also uses this image in *ZBA*, p. 140.
109. *NS*, p. 37.
110. *CMP*, p. 35; reprinted as *CP*, p. 23.
111. *ZBA*, pp. 72-73.
112. *NS*, p. 6.
113. *CMP*, p. 56; reprinted as *CP*, p. 40.
114. Merton, in the introduction to *The Monastic Theology of Aelred of Rievaulx*, p. xii.
115. *CWA*, p. 69.
116. *IE*, p. 15.
117. *CWA*, p. 61.
118. *IE*, p. 15.
119. Ibid., p. 16; this is Merton's paraphrase of Augustine.
120. Merton, *Disputed Questions* (New York: Farrar, Straus & Giroux, 1960), p. 123.

AUTHOR'S NOTE: *This chapter is difficult and technical. The general reader may wish to omit it.*

III

PERSONHOOD ACCORDING TO WALSH

WHO AM I? That is the fundamental question for Daniel Clark Walsh. Walsh's understanding of person does not refer to what distinguishes oneself from everyone else; rather the person in each expresses what all have in common: most simply, that all are loved by God.

Walsh sees the origin of persons as God's immediate experience of Himself as imitable, and that is the reason that person is not definable. Definition deals with essences, and Walsh sees the origin of the person as prior to generation of essences. Furthermore, Walsh understands definitions as dealing with *what* something is, not the *who* of personal reference.

Walsh tries to move away from what a person is to person as a relational reality, a relation constituted by God and for God; accordingly Walsh rejects the Boethian definition of person as individual substance of rational nature. The Boethian definition categorizes person as a type of being as distinguished from other types of being. Walsh views person in relation to God, that is, as image of God.

Walsh's understanding of person was accomplished by use of a number of contrasting distinctions. This method, which Walsh never labeled, I call polarity presentation.

Polarity presentation, that is, presentation of polar opposites relative to personal identity finds literary expression in Christianity as early as the New Testament. Paul, for example, opposes the notions of the old man and the new, the first Adam with the Second, the image of the man of dust with the image of the man of heaven, and living according to the flesh with living according to the Spirit. The synoptic Gospels, especially, express the paradoxical situation of having to lose one's life or self in order to gain it. Christian life, according to the synoptics, consists in this exchange of selves, or at least in living with the tension between them.

Daniel Clark Walsh speaks of this question of selfhood in terms of polarities other than the biblical polarities just mentioned. Walsh writes of person versus individual, and person versus nature. Although Christian theology has seen these terms as helpful for solving dogmatic disputes, in the thought of Walsh these terms are as vividly spiritual as the biblical categories. Walsh also uses the polarities of individuality versus uniqueness, and collectivity versus community. For those privileged to hear Walsh expound his personalistic spirituality, there were often moments of excitement and illumination. At the same time, however, Walsh could cause confusion and perplexity.

Many know of Daniel Clark Walsh through his relationship with Thomas Merton. Walsh and Merton met when Merton was a student at Columbia University and Walsh was teaching medieval philosophy as a visiting professor there. At that time he was a professor of philosophy at Manhattanville College of the Sacred Heart. Walsh had studied under Etienne Gilson and Jacques Maritain and received his doctorate at the Pontifical Institute of Medieval Studies at the University of Toronto.[1]

When Merton began thinking about the priesthood and religious life, he went to Walsh for advice. This meeting was the beginning of their long friendship. Around 1960, Walsh came to Kentucky to teach at the Abbey of Gethsemani and at nearby Loretto Junior College. He later taught at Bellarmine College in Louisville, and at 59, in 1967, he was ordained a Roman Catholic priest in Louisville. Abbot James Fox gave Merton permission to meet with Walsh each week, and they were able to continue their friendship and to develop together their Christian thought until Merton's death in 1968. Walsh died on the Feast of St. Augustine, August 28, 1975, and was buried at Gethsemani.

In his long teaching career, Walsh wrote relatively little. The student of Walsh has access to articles and transcriptions of talks that Walsh gave while living in Kentucky and several transcriptions of discussions that took place with some of the monks at the Abbey of Gethsemani. In addition, there is Walsh's doctoral dissertation and a series of cassette recordings of a course on medieval philosophy that Walsh gave at Bellarmine College.

Walsh's notion of the person, his central insight, provides a metaphysical foundation for Christian spirituality. Such a foundation is clearly needed in the contemporary Church, where both intellectual confusion and spiritual hunger are found at high levels. Walsh's notion of the person can also help the reader to understand Merton's thought on true versus false self.

Toward a Description of Person

THE PERSON IN WALSH'S PHILOSOPHY is an image of Trinitarian love. Walsh says that "the person is God expressed in the totality of his knowledge and love, that perfect image of God proceeding from the divine Trinity."[2] Personhood is not a static notion; it implies a process of perfection in love. Definitions tend to leave out the movement in existence.[3] The person is *who* we really are, not *what* we are, and therein lies the difficulty in trying to define person. Definitions deal with essences, but person is not an essence.

"Know thyself" is an injunction at the source of the mainstream philosophical and spiritual traditions of Greece, of Christianity, and of Hinduism. That the self cannot be observed as an object is evidence of a great mystery. Most people believe they know who they are, but those who take the trouble to disidentify with their own images of self, with their roles, come to understand that selfhood is hidden in a promising darkness. To investigate Walsh's notion of the person is to invite a knowledge of the truth of oneself and of one's union with God and all that is.

Origin of Person

WALSH ADMITS THAT his teaching on person is transphilosophical inasmuch as the Christian doctrine of the Trinity and the biblical idea of creation by God are foundational for his philosophy of person. To understand person, it is necessary to reflect upon the Holy Trinity and then upon the act of creation by the divine Trinity. A very brief statement of the Trinitarian activity will help readers to find their way through Walsh's descriptions below.

The Son is the Father's self-knowledge. The generation of the Son is the Father knowing Himself. The Son is the perfect knowledge of the Father; in that relation is total unconcealment, perfect transparency. In God, Walsh recognizes metaphysical moments so that he can posit that the act of the divine will follows the act of divine intellect; a thing must be known before it can be willed. With the generation of the Son in divine self-knowing, there arises "an immediate response of the Will of God in perfect Love."[4] The Holy Spirit is this divine Love. The divine Persons "subsist" as relations "within God to God . . . Knowing in the Father; Knowledge in the Son; Loving in both the Father and the Son; Love in the Holy Spirit."[5]

This description of Trinitarian life is not unusual. It is the kind of description one customarily finds in traditional Catholic theology. When Walsh describes the movement from within to outside of the Trinity in creation, he reveals the influence of Duns Scotus and gives a transphilosophical grounding for the person.

Divine Freedom

FROM DUNS SCOTUS, Walsh borrows the notion of *creabilia*, the creatable possibles that God sees in Himself. In the Word, all possible participants in God are seen, as are all theoretical principles. Thus "after" the generation of the Son and the processions of the Holy Spirit, God comprehends all possible imitations of Himself, the *creabilia*. These creatable intelligibles have no claim to existence. They are mere possibles generated in the divine intelligence. For these possibles to come into existence, they require a divine act of love; God must will them into existence. By the will of God creation is effected; God freely selects which of the possibles may come into existence.[6] The person is the perfection of knowledge and love that God sees in Himself prior to creation.[7] The person is an image of divine love. This perfection of divine love is not thought of as a substance but rather as subsisting relations.

In Walsh's doctoral dissertation "The Metaphysics of Ideas According to Duns Scotus," he emphasizes God's freedom. The divine intellect knows all necessary truths and all possible contingent truths prior to its act of will. The production of ideas, or essences, in God is not dependent upon the divine will. God's will chooses between possibles. Although volition follows intellection with regard to the future, nevertheless future contingents require a determining act of God's will in order for them to be known. Through the divine will, God determines which of a set of possibles presented by the intellect will become real. His movement relative to creatures is thoroughly free, hence all things are loved into being.

Walsh acknowledges what few philosophical Christian theologians would dispute: "Knowledge and love operate within the personal life of God."[8] He then goes on to distinguish between God's acts of knowing and loving and the objects of his knowing and loving:

> The intuition of knowledge and love as experience is incommunicable because it is person. What is formally communicated then is what is "in that knowledge" and "in that love" and this is creation from the standpoint of nature. Natural creation becomes somewhat intelligible when we see it as distinct from personal creation and I am not sure that this personal situation of which I speak can even legitimately be called a creation.[9]

God's incommunicable experience of Himself as imitable contains the ground for what Walsh calls person. Walsh here acknowledges that God's self knowledge, traditionally located in the Word, which includes possible imitations of Himself in other beings, is not identical with the objects of His knowledge even as forms or ideas in Himself. The divine intellect conceptualizes His relationship to Himself and to possibilities; this conceptualization is the generation of ideas.

Walsh distinguished this conceptualization from the prior intuition of God. The prior loving intuition of God is God's personal life; it is God's most intimate subjectivity without trace of otherness. This Walsh reluctantly calls "personal creation" because "creation" traditionally refers to what is other than God.

Walsh understands Christianity to be an invitation to share in the personal life of God, hence he sees human personhood to be a share in the divine intimacy prior to conceptualization in God. *Prior* is generally a temporal word; here, however, it means "more intimate" or "more central."

The above discussion links the personal with God's intuition and immediate experience; such immediate experience is incommunicable. What can be communicated is mediated through forms or ideas or essences. Walsh would not want to allow one to confuse immediate personal experience with an idea. Personhood underlies anything that can be objectivized in an essence, even in God's mind. The person originates in God's experience of Himself as imitable. This level in God is the ground for the personal in human images of God. This personal level cannot be captured totally in ideas, since it is prior to ideas. Expression of experience in communicable forms is the level of nature that Walsh will not allow to be confused with the level of person.

The human person reflects divine relatedness. As Walsh says,

> The person in whose image all men and all angels are created subsists primarily in the noetic of divine knowledge. This image reflects the *Logos* and fore-

shadows the person in every existing man and every angel whose total subsistence is in the noetic of love.[10]

In the perfect image, God saw the perfection of the person, and God wills the perfection of every person.[11] "The model God looked to in our creation was not primarily the Divine Idea of man, eternally in God's Word, but rather the *Word* of God Himself, the Second Person of the Blessed Trinity Who is Christ."[12] In other words, God's precognition of the person is principally His self-knowledge. Thus the divine knowledge of created persons originates in His self-knowledge and includes intentional knowledge of perfection of persons. This latter intentional knowledge must carry a note of otherness but without losing the subjective pole of Divine self-knowledge. God knows created persons both objectively and subjectively, that is, center to center.

Boethius Rejected

WALSH REJECTS THE BOETHIAN DEFINITION of the human person as individual substance of a rational nature.[13] His basis for going beyond the Boethian definition is that Boethius focuses on the nature, which for Walsh is not sufficiently primordial. Walsh locates the origin of the person in what he calls personal creation — that is, in God's self-determination. Persons originate in the Logos as imitations, or reflections, of God's relation to Himself.[14]

To focus on individuality, substantiality, or rationality, as does the Boethian definition, is to pass over the intimate relationship with God that makes person to be person. As Walsh puts it,

> To be a person FIRST means "to be made in the image and likeness of God." Now the perfect Image of God is Christ, the second Person of the Blessed Trinity. A created person is one *who* is made in this Image and the end for which the person is created is to manifest the Truth of Christ in the love God has for Himself in His Divine Trinity.[15]

To be a person is to image God's relation to Himself. To try to translate person into the categories of Aristotle, as Boethius and others did, is to omit the origin and end of person in God's inner life. The religious import of this move away from definition of person as individual or substantial or rational is that person as a term contains a direct reference to God.

Priority of Person

"NATURE," FOR WALSH, DENOTES the order of creation or the beings within that order.[16] Walsh's emphasis is on the distinction between person and nature.

Logically, since both angels and humans have different natures, what makes them persons cannot be defined by their natures. The distinction between person and nature in Walsh's thought agrees with classical Christology. "If the person as such is not distinct from the nature," Walsh writes, "then the Divine person of the Son could not take on the human nature of Christ."[17]

Walsh takes the terminological distinction from classical Christology and focuses upon the person as grounded in a Christocentric view of creation, that is, with Christ as Logos. In God's relationship with Himself is personal life. That personal life is imaged in created persons, whatever their nature — human or angelic. This distinction between person and nature enables Walsh to allow for a developmental dimension to person; development is through nature.[18]

Personal identity is primarily the relation of each person to the Divine Image. The will and intellect of every person is perfected in the relation of the person to Christ ("I live, not I, but Christ lives in me"). This is spiritual formation in its philosophical foundation. There was spiritual formation before the creation of any nature — so that, the intellect and will of the person refer primarily to "intellect and will in God." Then to the intellect and will embodied in the person through the nature in creation. That is, the creation of things in their own genera and species follows upon this personal formation in being.[19]

Walsh thus envisions personal creation prior to creation embodied in nature. Personal creation implies a share in God's intimate life in the Logos. This intimacy is objectified in the mind of God as possible imitations of Him. By His creative and utterly free act of will, these possibles are given existence in nature:

> What does the notion of nature add to all this? We might say that nature is simply the divine order of things in being. The "to be" of things is the principle of their existence in an orderly relation to one another and all in relation to the end of all. (*Inter sese et ad finem.*) Things are related to one another in different ways; nature assigns to each kind of being its place in the order of being. The extension of personal creation into nature was fittingly proposed in the noetic of knowledge and ontologically ratified in the noetic of love. The highest beings are those closest to the creation of the first intellectual nature, and the lowest those farthest removed from it. So that, when the person was called into existence and given a nature, it was simply being assigned its place in created being.[20]

The order of beings in relation to each other and to their end is nature for Walsh. Nature is the arena for the personal life God wills to share. Persons as images of God are equipped with natures, angelic or human, in order to actualize the intentions of God. Thus nature in addition to being an orderly arrangement is linked to actualizing potential.

Persons originate and end in God; they are given natures consisting of body and soul[21] in order to perfect their potential to love as God loves. Nature with the help of grace "is intended for one end — to fulfill and complete the person in the one God calls into created existence."[22] Here Walsh's emphasis in describing the person is on finality.

God is related to all beings, for He has loved them into existence. All existents are not necessarily relating to God. Persons are related to God by their love; personal creation involves the constituting of loving relations and the potential for such love. One may take a lifetime to actualize fully the potential for love.

Walsh sees the human likeness to God primarily in the order of the person rather than in the order of nature, for, as Walsh says, "there is personal life alone in God — there is no nature. How could there be since nature is a principle of limit and God is infinite. Nature is always finite."[23] Personal identity is one's likeness to God; the identity established by one's nature is merely identity in relation to natural creation.[24]

Walsh's stress on person over nature shows his point of reference to be God as Creator and Christ as Logos. Walsh also admits that through the assumption of human nature by the Logos, human nature is divinized. In the Incarnation one may see the way person and nature fit together. According to Walsh,

> the person in man . . . is always "godlike" — the nature only became godlike when it was assumed by Christ — it was divinely personalized but it remained human — and through our transformation in it, we became adopted sons of God. Human nature is not only restored; it is also re-created — and the new man in us takes on a nature that is divinely personalized.[25]

Nature is tied to action. The person in a human being can use his or her nature for selfishness or for service to God.[26] Walsh sees divine love operating through the activities of human nature. He says that "we should never think of natures as static. . . . Rather we should think of them as dynamic principles operating in an order that has for its first principle Love. . . ."[27]

Walsh sees Divine love as leading human persons beyond their natures. "In man," he writes, "this nature is prolonged into the supernatural — the same order devoted to a new mode of existence — a love that unites man to all the things above him in his nature but not above him in his person. . . ."[28]

Walsh does not want to deprecate nature by distinguishing between nature and person and by emphasizing the priority of the person. He sees the distinction as ennobling nature by showing that the true intention of nature is "to fulfill and complete the person in the one God calls into created existence.[29] Person is an "end in itself," whereas nature is a means for the perfection of the person.[30]

Though Walsh speaks of going beyond nature through supernatural elevation, he emphasizes that the person is a natural effusion of God's love. The person is linked with God's originating call into existence. Thus Walsh does not exalt redemption or the supernatural, for he sees in nature evidence of the greatest love. Persons naturally arise in the unity of God's self-diffusive love:

> The highest dignity that can come to man is that of the first love. The greatest of loves — nothing can exceed it — is the love of God in creating you. Nothing, no love, is higher than that. Even the love with which God saves us in redemption is a kind of "forced" love, not an absolutely free love.[31]

Personhood naturally and by definition relates to God. The supernatural is God's way of restoring or repairing what has gone wrong. "The love of God," says Walsh, "is natural to man."[32]

Person and Individual

WALSH'S TEACHING ON THE PRIORITY of person over nature derives from his Trinitarian starting point:

> When God said let *us* make man in *our* image . . . , this is obviously God speaking to us in his Trinity and it would seem that the "image" of which God speaks was already present. God saw or was seeing the image and all of us in it, which means also that he did not first see us in the "nature of man" . . . He was seeing us in the likeness of the Trinity — the personal life of God.[33]

God's vision of human beings begins in the Logos. He "sees" humans within Himself prior to seeing humans in their own natures. Nature, according to Walsh, is "but the external expressions of God's will."[34]

An implication of the priority of person over nature is that human individuals are constituted in existence within their individual natures. Humans, understood as individuals, are humans viewed through their natures.

Walsh's most developed thought on the person-versus-individual distinction occurs in two of a series of discussions held at the Abbey of Gethsemani in the early 1970s. These discussions among Walsh's friends (mostly monks of Gethsemani) were designed to evoke Walsh's teaching, which was usually communicated orally. Walsh's health had been failing. Thus, to prevent his thought on the person from being lost, the discussions were recorded and transcribed.

In one of these discussions Walsh states explicitly what was only hinted at earlier: "The individual is related to the nature, not to the person. The person is related to God."[35] That which is like God in us is our person; that which is not godlike pertains to our individuality.

In another of these discussions at Gethsemani, Walsh distinguished between person and individual, but in doing so, he introduces the note of necessity:

> The ego, the individual ego, would be what we call the individual, this physical man, necessarily implying space and time and place, whereas the person does not. The person is a relationship to God which is transcendental. So, it's in being, the person is always in being because it's a relationship to God who is, He who is, the eternal being. Therefore, the person is involved in this eternal order of things which is divine, but on a natural level, not a supernatural level. So there is a divine natural relationship to God (by which) we are necessarily related to God in being. In the individual, we are not; we're contingent, in the contingent order. Thus, the individual comes into existence which is temporal and leaves this temporal existence, is born and dies. The person is neither born nor does the person die. . . . The person is a transcendental relation, which means an eternal relation to God which God establishes before everything else.

Then He brings the physical order into being, says, "Let it be." The physical order is something God has decreed by an order of free decisions — absolutely free decisions because absolutely contingent upon the free will of God. The person is not contingent. The person is the necessary emanation of God's love. God's love is necessary to God. He could not be without his love, so that all God loves is necessarily founded on the very being of God, on God Himself. But the contingent order of existence is founded on the free will of God.[36]

These passages raise difficulties in reconciling Walsh's thought with Christian orthodoxy, to which he felt a strong allegiance. Traditionally, Christianity maintains that creation is contingent, not necessary to God, in order to affirm the divine self-sufficiency. Here, however, Walsh says that the person is "not contingent" but is "the necessary emanation of God's love." Does Walsh mean to say that persons are not part of creation?

There are two likely explanations for the above. The first is that person *as person* is a concept univocally applied to God and creatures. Person *as person* is neither divine nor human, but person is qualified by the nature. Person as person is not part of creation, but person *as human* is.[37] This explanation is likely because it expresses the thinking of Duns Scotus, whose thought Walsh studied and taught for most of his adult life.

The second explanation, which follows, is preferable because it is simpler and avoids the application of the technical notion of univocity to Walsh's concept, which he never explicitly used. *Person*, as Walsh uses the term, primarily refers to divine Person. As the above quotation says, person is "an eternal relation to God." Person is a divine reality that can be reflected in the created order. The primary meaning of person transcends the created order, since it is "an external relation to God." That relation to God can be extended to creatures who can image relationship with God within the restrictions of their nature.

Both of these explanations are compatible with Walsh's

statement that person is not contingent. What is contingent is the establishment of human nature as a vehicle for relationship with God.

What *person* means here is God's relationship to Himself in love; such a relation is necessary, since that is God's identity. Walsh contrasts the contingent order with that which is generated in God's experience of Himself:

> Contingent existence will run its course, eventually to return to the nothing whence it came. But the existence of that which is in the power of God's love remains forever. It began with God to remain with God for all eternity.[38]

Created persons are possible participations in God's personal life. I use the term *possible* to acknowledge that human persons, passing through the contingent order of nature, may not actualize God's intention. Person as relationship with God is an eternal act in God as well as an eternal intention, hence possibility, in humans and angels.

Above, Walsh simply states that "the person is always in being because it's a relationship to God who is." Walsh uses the present tense in order to emphasize that the person is an eternal relationship with God in God. Humans and angels have personhood as their eternal home, which they enter through the door of contingency, possibility, created nature, individuality.

Before going further into how individuality fits into Walsh's vision, the implications of the above relative to love and the person need comment. The person is loved, by definition, prior to and apart from any consideration of contingency. The love operating in God is necessary, and created persons are called to share in that love. In addition, persons, as Walsh states above, "in the contingent order of existence," are loved in virtue of God's creative freedom.

Individuality carries mainly a negative connotation for Walsh. His pejorative use of the term *individual* is linked to a pejorative understanding of the empirical ego. As the passages above show, Walsh contrasts person as a necessary and transcendental relation to God with the individual or individual ego — which implies limitations of the physical, namely, space and time. These limitations mean that the individual is temporary.

Walsh adds to this pejorative view of individuality by introducing the ideas of separation and self-creation:

> The individual is a separation, is self-created, made himself. When Adam separated himself from God, he became an individual in the true sense of separation. So an individual is someone separated from the unity in which he has the frutition of his being. Matter is the principle of this, so God created matter as something which would provide for man's restoration. He's given us this to start the work back.[39]

Walsh here says that individuality and materiality result from the fall of Adam. Such a view presumes that Adam preexisted the material order. Such a view harmonizes with persons as eternal relations.

What is especially regretable, however, about this utterance of Walsh's is that material creation becomes intrinsically linked to the Fall and Redemption rather than simply giving scope to divine love. This view of Walsh's would make material existence and individuality mere launchpads for one's heavenly home. The otherworldliness of this view is undeniable, as is the deprecation of individuality.

Probably in order to prevent Walsh from resting in this pejorative view of human individuality, Father Tarcisius, in the same group discussion, offers a lifeline:

> One thing I found helpful in this same line was the idea of comparing this with the way the Fathers spoke of image and resemblance. The image is given by God at the beginning; the resemblance, perfection, is at the end. Both are really the person. Your individual then becomes the vehicle by which you pass from one to the other.

Walsh responds to this comment affirmatively, "Yes."[40] That affirmation goes undeveloped. After the yes, Walsh adds, "That's why He allowed himself to be born: to restore, establish, confirm that."⁴¹ If the transcriber correctly capitalized *He*, then Walsh is saying that God in Christ took flesh, or entered human existence, to restore humanity to its right relation with God. Christ thus ratifies the usefulness of material existence in restoring fallen humanity to its true personal relationship with God.

The positive meaning of individuality is thus the arena for restoration or reformation. In addition, one can say from the above that Walsh agrees with Tarcisius' remark that person may be expressed through individuality.

Earlier in the discussions, Walsh again responds to Tarcisius' suggestion that "the individual always has to contain and express something of the person, though he never contains it fully."⁴² Walsh's response is:

> That's right. And that's why we, as individuals, form this community that tries to express the person. The more they are one and not many, the more they are that person whom God created in the beginning. That's why you don't count persons.⁴³

Here Walsh's admission that person may be expressed through the individual is hardly flattering for individuality. Ultimately the manyness of individuals is to be transcended, hence individuality with its manyness appears to be a temporary stepping-stone at best.

Individuality and Uniqueness

WALSH'S PEJORATIVE USE of the term *individual* may strike the Christian reader as peculiar in light of Walsh's Christian commitment. Is not Christianity a religion derived from individual events? Clearly the quest for unity dominates Walsh's thought, and that unity unfortunately can give the impression of swallowing up individuality. While individuality carries largely negative connotations for Walsh, the undeniably multiple face of reality receives his positive acknowledgement under the term *uniqueness*.

The Person is the common basis for personal communication among persons in the spiritual life of man, and this is the Divine Image according to which we are created and conformed to Christ as persons — a person is a unique conformity to Christ.[44]

Above we have seen Walsh refer to individuality in terms of contingency, limitation, and self-centered separation. Now he refers to persons as a "unique conformity to Christ." How can Walsh bemoan individuality and honor uniqueness? If one emphasizes "conformity to Christ," one will avoid claiming contradiction. A person is unique; each person is an unrepeatable expression of divine creativity. A person is a unique relationship with God emanating from His relationship with Himself, which is Person with a capital letter. The divine intention for creating persons is that they fully enter into His personal life, which means conformity to Christ, who is God's personal life perfectly expressed.

Individual human nature provides the context for conformity to Christ. Individuality is not an end in itself. If however, one lives in order to accent how one differs from others, one's orientation is disordered. To focus upon one's own image is not the divine intention; rather, to focus on the divine Image who is Christ is the way of the person. The latter orientation ratifies one's uniqueness and leads to a unity within God's personal life. In the concrete, people are individuals and persons; the terms *unique* and *separate* describe positive and negative poles of human existence.

Person and Community

THE GETHSEMANI DIALOG "Person and Community I," which gives Walsh's most developed thought on the person versus individual distinction also gives Walsh's thinking about community. Collectivity corresponds to individual, and person corresponds to community.[45] A collection of individuals who merely assert their undividedness does not contain the self-transcending dynamic necessary for true community. Relatedness to God is Walsh's hope for a genuine community insofar as such a community may reflect God's unconditional love, however imperfectly. Individuality can at best lead to collectivity when individuality is not expressive of the person. Personhood, on the other hand, is synonymous with communion. Walsh understands the development of true community as centered in conscious loving relationship with God: "What must come first is the consciousness of being loved, as God loves us, then we'd be conscious of loving ourselves, that we're lovable. We must be lovable before we can love even ourselves."[46] Self-love is a function of accepting God's acceptance of oneself. If one enters a Christian community as a person who is loved by God and called to live with others, then that community is the divinely provided environment. This is what Walsh means when he says that the community exists "for you."

> To know that the community exists for you is to know that you are worth what the community exists for. In other words, the community wouldn't exist for you unless it be in the nature of things that this be so. When you become conscious of that . . . you become conscious of the fact you're the risen Christ.[47]

The introduction of the idea of the risen Christ is merely an echo of Walsh's foundation of the person in the Logos. One's beginning, end, and true identity on earth are in the Word.

The danger of thinking that the community exists "for you" is in identifying "you" with the individual. In order to guard against this misunderstanding, Walsh takes his statement that the community exists for you and inverts it by saying that you exist for the community. "He [someone] has to be acceptable to accept the fact that he exists for the community."[48]

Does Walsh mean that a human being exists for the community or vice versa? Walsh affirms both. The community is given to the human being for the human being's development. The human being is given to the community to help to realize its true end, which is the life of charity. The human being who selfishly uses the community subordinates the person to the individual. The individual needs to enter the circle of love in order for the person in the individual to be manifest and in order for the personal love of God to be realized in the group.

The community of persons in Christ about which Walsh speaks is far deeper than togetherness.

> To see unity, this great unity, in the many, to see the One is much more difficult than to see the One in the One. It's a great challenge: you have to fight to be one in many. You have to undergo a trial, suffer with Christ.[49]

Walsh links suffering with "seeing" the One in the many. The type of seeing that involves suffering is faith in the person. To relate to others exclusively on the basis of personality differences is to fail to understand the other as called by God. To intuit the person in the other implies a letting go of whatever in oneself interferes with loving the other. Such detachment and willingness to change is the suffering implied in genuine Christian community. Walsh acknowledges contemplation,[50] or seeing "the One in the One," and solitude[51] as necessary components for the ability to "see" the person in the other, hence for the formation and functioning of genuine Christian community.

Natural Basis for Spirituality

WALSH'S PHILOSOPHY IS in service of truth — more specifically, of Christian truth; and Christian truth is in service of Christian life. His notion of the person is replete with spiritual implications. Walsh recognizes in the person a natural basis for spirituality, and his thought and discussion about the person are more a metaphysical meditation than an exercise in philosophical rigor.

Spirituality implies a relationship with a transcendent reality. In Walsh's philosophy, this relationship is central. The relation of love is the person. The effusion of divine love constitutes divine, angelic, and human persons. This outpouring of love is natural to God, who is Love, and the love of God is thus natural to all persons, since personhood is constituted in that love.

One's origin in divine love is deeper than anything in one's nature, even than one's individuality. One's deepest and truest identity is found in relation to His love. Furthermore, one's end, the finality that guides one's ordered actions, is the perfect realization of His intention.

Person as End

THE SPIRITUALITY OF PERSON highlights the dynamic element in personal life. Person is an eternal relationship, yet created persons have to actualize that relationship through time.

There is almost no secondary literature on Walsh, but a talk by Fr. Flavian Burns, who was abbot of Gethsemani when Walsh died, contributes to the understanding of person as end. Walsh admitted that Fr. Flavian was one of those who best understood what he meant by person. Burns speaks of person in terms of finality; person, in Aristotelian language, is the final cause of the human being. Burns offers a capsule-sized analysis in terms of Aristotle's four chief causes. Formal cause: rational; material cause: animal; and efficient cause: God creating. Like Walsh, Burns sees final cause as person.[52] Humans are called to be persons in God's overarching plan to unite all things in Himself.

As noted above, natures are given to persons; persons, however, are ends rather than means.[53] Persons in Walsh's scheme are prior to all of physical creation so that the true order would not subjugate persons to what is created for the sake of persons. Human beings may or may not enter into personal relationship with God. To enter into a personal relationship with God, a human being must be responsive to God's call, to the gift of love that constitutes his or her own reality.

> All of us are called to do whatever we are given to do in the best possible way. You know you're acting

in accordance with the will of God when you're not only baking bread but baking the best bread you know how to bake or writing the best essay you know how to write.[54]

Thus Walsh envisions personal development in terms of the call of God and responsiveness to that call. The call of God is synonymous with person; one originates in that call and is guided by that call toward progressive conformity into the likeness of Christ. To regard person as final cause is to bring up the question of whether one is a person now or only at the end of one's life. Each person *as* a person, is an intention of God, who gives existence to His intentions in order that His love may be imaged. The principal meaning of person is God's own life; created persons are actualizations of divine intentionality through Love's response to love. The Person is the perfect image of God, and created persons bear that image. One's personhood is in one's progressively more perfect resemblance to that image.[55]

Faith

THE WAY OF REALIZATION is through faith. Walsh contrasts faith with vision:

> The knowledge and love of God in faith had simply to wait upon the knowledge and love of God in vision. Men and angels were asked to persevere in faith in order to be confirmed as persons in Heaven. The grace to persevere in faith is the prelude to its confirmation in the final grace of sanctifying vision.[56]

Thus faith is a way of knowing. This involves understanding self as person, since

> the act of faith is man's acknowledgement and agreement that he has been, from time immemorial, encased in the love of God revealed to him, and this faith comprises everything in the historical sphere

that the believer encounters *a posteriori* as facts of revelation.[57]

Thus faith is a reference to one's origin and an orientation guided by one's end in God. The metaphysical basis for the operation of faith is one's origin in the Logos. What Walsh calls "primordial faith"[58] is a participation in God's own self-knowledge. Faith is the intelligibility of one's relationship with God.

The person, for Walsh, is revealed by faith. While one may find in the philosophical traditions of the West person defined as individual substance of rational nature, it is important to go beyond such a limited horizon to glimpse the true end of human beings. That end is union with God; faith communicates the truth of the origin and end of the human.[59] Faith gives the most adequate perspective for personal human life, since personal life is rooted in God. Through faith in their predestination for full participation in Trinitarian life, persons are able to rise above rationality and to orient their individuality toward a union with all in love. Without faith there would be no Christian personalism.

Prayer

WALSH DOES NOT DEVELOP much thought explicitly on prayer, though all of his personalistic thought easily adapts into reflections on prayer.

Faith is a door to the knowledge of the truth of one's personal origin and end; such knowledge begins prayer in the wakeful heart. To know that a person issues from an overflow of divine love and is given existence by a free choice of God in order that one may enter His life fully is to know oneself as embraced. To recognize all of a person's life as a flow from the divine goodness is to open the door of the heart to gratitude and praise, and to urge one to make one's feeble attempt to return something of the riches He has given. From the moment we awaken to our Creator, we are compelled to admit that we are debtors. As a grateful debtor, a person cannot communicate his or her entire being in one act. The approach of death tells each of us that we cannot help but fail to repay the Lord for His goodness. In this poverty, faith tells us that each of us is more than a debtor: we are sons and daughters. The awareness of being held in being by God, the awareness that all is gift, that each of us is a debtor and a pauper, that each of us is a beloved son or daughter — such are the seeds of contemplation.

Prayer is the awareness of His love. The person is an articulation of the relationship that generates the Christian spiritual life. Prayer is also a person's openness to God as one's future. Whatever limitations one encounters, a person's spirit points one beyond them all; prayer is the voice of faith, hope, and love, and these endure when everything else passes away. Though earthly life contains countless disappointments, one's human spirit, oriented in personal relation with God, carries one's self-understanding beyond ordinary limitation. Prayer is an awakening to the person — that is, to one's origin and end in the love of God.

Clarifications

A MAJOR DIFFICULTY with speaking of the metaphysical priority of person is that the impression can be given that person and nature are separable. A related issue is how one can distinguish persons from subhuman beings if person means relatedness to God. How is a human being a person but a flower not? To answer this question, one needs to refer to the origin of the person, to the nature given to the person, and to the end of the person.

The origin of the person is God's incommunicable experience of himself as imitable. Persons thus imitate, or image, God's inner life. To understand that imitation, one must point to knowing and loving in relation to God to arrive at the person. In other words, human nature seems to be necessary to distinguish between those beings loved by God that are not persons and those that are.

Reference to such notions as uniqueness and individuality as developed above will help in distinguishing person from subpersons. The first point brings out the uniqueness of person in relation to God. Walsh says, "There's one nature and will in all men. Besides this there's a personal will, unique in each of us."[60] Thus Walsh distinguishes nature as a common metaphysical reality for all human beings from the unique will in each, which he calls "personal."

One's personal will is personal, not simply because it is individual, but because it emerges from unique relatedness to God and is actualized in relatedness to God through one's nature. Any common component of humanity that one may select does not specify the source, way, and end of human existence in relation to God.

The other point that will clarify this question of distinguishing person from other beings loved by God comes from the nature-person distinction. The person can transcend human nature through grace.[61] The individual human nature that one has may be moved beyond its ordinary sluggishness to a more Christlike life. Thus, person as subject of grace is person as subject in relation to God. Divine influence can energize one's will, can elevate one's nature. Divine influence can move a person beyond his or her nature in beatific vision. Such a transcendent experience is personal yet beyond nature. Person thus signifies relatedness to God, God as source, way, and end of existence.

We can now say how one may determine how a flower or other subhuman being is not a person. A flower is loved into being, but a flower is not intended by God to share in His life. The human person is intended for, guided to, and fulfilled in relation to God. A human person needs a human nature in order to respond to God's creative love. Free will is part of an individual's human nature. The proper finality of that freedom is personal life with God.

Personal life is through human nature, but human nature does not originate the divinely intended direction of a human being. The person is the reflection of divine will in the human will. The human will is needed to actualize the divine will, but the human will or human nature on its own does not denote relation to God.

Both a flower and a human being are loved into being, and they obviously differ in nature. But Walsh would also point to the personal dimension of a human which is its source, way, and end in God.

If one locates freedom in human nature, does it follow that freedom is neither a component of the person nor of the image of God? Nature and person are two aspects of one human being. Free will as part of human nature is a faculty within human psychology; this faculty is abstracted by that science through analysis. Free will oriented to God is a fulfilling of the divine intention and as such is an activity of the person.

Through Walsh's understanding of person, Christian spirituality is given a notion that transcends human nature yet allows for the immanence of a self deeper than individuality. The Walshian view of person calls into question one's self-understanding in order to trigger awareness of one's identity in relation to God.

Walsh justifies his distinctions between person and individual in terms of the Trinitarian theological tradition and classical Christology. The concepts of person and individual are not identical in classical theology, but there is an underlying justification of this distinction that is implicit in Walsh's thought. The distinctions between person and individual, person and nature, individuality and uniqueness, and collectivity and community aim to help one to question one's identity, relationships, and orientation. Ordinary English usage allows for equivalent meanings for each term in each pair; for example, *individual* equals *person* in common parlance. Such verbal equivalence corresponds to a psychological identification, and human fulfillment becomes identified with ego gratification. Walsh's distinctions have a therapeutic effect in that they call into question one's identity and point to the possibility for life in union with God.

Walsh provides a concept, the person, that enables people of prayer to think out their relation to God in terms of identity. Their thought on identity will be protected from the self-centered ideology of the "me" generation and will be in harmony with the New Testament call to transformation. In addition, the Walsh language rejuvenates language that is already part of the Christian, Catholic, and contemplative traditions.

NOTES FOR CHAPTER III

1. A short chronology from Daniel Clark Walsh's "Programme of the Final Oral Examination for the Degree of Doctor of Philosophy," University of Toronto, School of Graduate Studies, May 19, 1934:
   1907   Born, Scranton, Pa.
   1930   B.A., U. of Toronto
   1930-31   M.A., U. of Toronto
   1931-32   Graduate School, U. of Toronto
   1932-33   Instructor in philosophy to Sisters of Mercy, Holy Spirit School, Atlantic City, N.J.
   1933-34   Graduate School, U. of Toronto; instructor in philosophy, St. Michael's College.

2. Daniel Clark Walsh, philosophy conference given at the Abbey of Gethsemani, June 2, 1966; p. 3.

3. Walsh, "Person and Community I," group discussion, Abbey of Gethsemani, November 6, 1971; p. 9.

4. Walsh, "Some Intimations," p. 7.

5. Ibid.

6. Walsh, "Anselm and Duns Scotus on Faith and the Person." Paper given at the Catholic University, 1966; pp. 8-12.

7. Ibid.

8. Walsh, "Anselm and Duns Scotus on Faith and the Person," p. 14.

9. Ibid.

10. From cassette no. 14 of Walsh's Bellarmine College course in medieval philosophy; Abbey of Gethsemani Library.

11. Walsh, "Anselm and Duns Scotus on Faith and the Person," pp. 15-16.

12. Ibid., p. 18.

13. Walsh, "Some Intimations," p. 15; also Walsh's Duns Scotus lecture given at St. Mary's, Kentucky, 1964, p. 7.

14. Walsh, "Anselm and Duns Scotus on Faith and the Person," pp. 14-16.

15. Walsh, "Some Intimations," pp. 14-15.

16. This understanding is in harmony with that of Thomas Aquinas, who, after acknowledging that there are a variety of meanings for nature, includes "substance" as a meaning. *Summa Theoloqiae*, I-II, Q.10, 1. He sees nature as principle of movement in *Summa Theoloqiae*, I-II, Q.58.

17. Walsh, "Three Conferences: On the Philosophy of Man and the Universal Society," Abbey of Gethsemani, p. 6, n.d.

18. Walsh, "Some Intimations," p. 17.

19. Walsh, "Anselm and Duns Scotus on Faith and the Person," p. 19.

20. Ibid.,
21. In "Some Intimations," Walsh acknowledges the Aristotelian definition of human nature: "man in his nature is defined as rational animal," p. 17.
22. Walsh, chapter talk, Abbey of Gethsemani, Sept. 1966, p. 2.
23. Walsh, chapter talk, Sept. 1966, p. 1.
24. Walsh, "Anselm and Duns Scotus on Faith and the Person," p. 23.
25. Ibid.
26. Ibid.
27. Walsh, "Some Intimations," p. 11.
28. Ibid.
29. Walsh, chapter talk, Sept. 1966, p. 2.
30. Walsh, "Anselm and Duns Scotus on Faith and the Person," p. 22.
31. Walsh, "Person and Community I," p. 2.
32. From cassette no. 14 from Walsh's Bellarmine course on medieval philosophy.
33. Walsh, chapter talk, Abbey of Gethsemani, June 1966, p. 3.
34. Walsh, "Three Conferences: On the Philosophy of Man and Universal Society," p. 4.
35. Walsh, "Person and Community II," group discussion, Abbey of Gethsemani, November 12, 1971; p. 4.
36. Walsh, "Person and Community I," pp. 1-2.
37. Walsh, "Person and Community II," p. 3.
38. Walsh, "Anselm and Duns Scotus on Faith and the Person," p. 14.
39. Walsh, "Person and Community I," pp. 5-6.
40. Ibid., p. 6.
41. Ibid.
42. Ibid., p. 4.
43. Ibid.
44. Walsh, chapter talk, Abbey of Gethsemani, March 1966, p. 2. See also Walsh, "Some Intimations," p. 6, for similar usage.
45. Walsh, "Person and Community I," p. 1.
46. Ibid., p. 7.
47. Ibid.
48. Ibid.
49. Ibid., p. 10.
50. Ibid., p. 9.

51. Ibid., p. 10.
52. Cassette of Fr. Flavian Burns, OCSO, on Walsh; Abbey of Gethsemani, August 28, 1976.
53. Walsh, "Anselm and Duns Scotus on Faith and the Person," p. 24.
54. Walsh, "Person and Community I," pp. 11-12.
55. Walsh, philosophy conference given at the Abbey of Gethsemani, June 2, 1966; pp. 3-4.
56. Walsh, "Anselm and Duns Scotus on Faith and the Person," p. 24.
57. Ibid., p. 4.
58. Ibid., p. 22.
59. Walsh, philosophy conference, June 2, 1966; p. 3.
60. Walsh, "Person and Nature in Augustine," cassette no. 72 of the Abbey of Gethsemani's "Merton tapes," September 3, 1963.
61. Walsh, chapter talk given at the Abbey of Gethsemani, September 1966, p. 2.

IV

MERTON AND WALSH

IT CANNOT BE ESTABLISHED with certainty exactly how much of Merton's understanding of person is taken from Walsh. What is evident is that they enriched one another over the many years of their friendship. The following segment of a dialog between Daniel Walsh and Fr. Flavian Burns is an explicit acknowledgment of Walsh's influence on Merton.

FLAVIAN: How much of Merton's thought about the self did he get from you?

DAN: I don't know. We'd been talking about that for years and years.

FLAVIAN: Those writing theses say Merton got his concept of the self and the deeper self and person from Maritain and Gilson.

DAN: Oh, it's far from that.

FLAVIAN: Only a few references in *Seven Storey Mountain* to the fact he's getting anything from Dan Walsh. If you've been exposed to Dan's thing on the person, it's clear that either you have the same source or you are the source.

DAN: I think it grew out of his studies when he was introduced to Scotus in my course. We at once got into a conflict of ideas, exchanged after the lectures.

It was Greek Fathers, through Scotus, who opened the thing to me, and I think it probably opened it up to him at the same time.

FLAVIAN: Your notion of person shed a lot of light on things mystics were saying. Fact there's no human person in Christ goes along with what Eckhart says mystics should do: get rid of ego so there's perfect openness to Word. We do this through identification with Christ. In relation to others we complement one another. Came to a head in Thomas Merton's writings while Dan was here and they had weekly discussions.

DAN: There was an influence, and he recognized it too.[1]

What is especially significant about this exchange is that the two men who knew Merton most intimately agree about the mutual influence. Father Flavian, Merton's last abbot and confessor, was closer to the mature Merton on the spiritual level than any other human being. Flavian begins with a question about Merton's source for his thinking on selfhood. The quotation is from a transcript of a dialog at which I was present, hence I can help the reader to see beyond the text. Flavian believed Walsh to be an important influence on Merton and felt that Walsh's influence was not being acknowledged by people unfamiliar with the Walsh-Merton relationship.

One result of this dialog was to evoke from Walsh an explicit statement concerning his presumed influence on Merton. Walsh, who was more intimate with Merton on the intellectual level than any other human being, acknowledges his influence on Merton's thinking about self. At the same time, Walsh admits a common element in the development of their thought on the person. He says he does not know exactly how much came from himself, as both he and Merton had been discussing personhood together for many years.

To buttress the emphasis that Walsh gives to their discussions, I add the observation that Walsh, in discussing the meaning of person, occasionally refers to Merton.[2] Although he may have introduced Merton to personalistic thinking, Walsh refers to Merton's writings when he wants to substantiate the points he is making for people more familiar with Merton's writing than his own. If Merton is quoted by Walsh, one can hardly characterize their mature relationship as teacher-student.

Merton uses the nature-person and individual-person distinctions, but he does not give detailed metaphysical bases for such distinctions. Merton addresses himself to a wide public, many of whom would not respond to theological technicalities; thus his lack of metaphysical language is understandable. And while similar distinctions can be found in the writings of Jacques Maritain, Flavian and Walsh agree that Maritain is not the source of such distinctions in Merton.

Though Merton and Walsh share a common language of the person, Merton's preferred language is "true" versus "false" self. Despite the substantial agreement between the two thinkers, one must examine Merton's use of person language prior to examining the true-self-versus-false-self polarity, for two reasons. First of all, the term *person* is the linguistic link with Walsh. Second, the word *person* resonates with Trinitarian language, which undergirds some of Merton's thought.

Merton's most explicit and developed thought on the person occurs in *New Seeds of Contemplation* and *Zen and the Birds of Appetite*. His personalistic thought, however, permeates much of his writings.[3] To the polarities of nature-person, individual-person, uniqueness-individuality and collectivity-community, Merton adds his own: true self versus false self; and true selfhood versus Cartesian selfhood.[4] The substantial agreement between Merton and Walsh on the meaning of person is substantial despite slight differences, which will be noted.

Origin of Person

WALSH GIVES DETAILED TREATMENT of the origin of person in God's incommunicable experience of Himself as imitable.

Merton does not give such detailed and technical discussion, although he refers to God as Trinity when discussing human personhood. He also emphasizes, in a way similar to Walsh, that one's identity is to be found in a relationship with God. Where Walsh gives a more metaphysical presentation, Merton's writings rely more on his own experiences.

The personhood of God is the human answer to a search that is filled with both darkness and confident hope. The purification that a contemplative undergoes involves letting go of all idolatrous handles. Progressively in prayer, a person allows God to be God by not reducing Him to something that fits comfortably within the human intellect.

> In the end the contemplative suffers the anguish of realizing that *he no longer knows what God is*. He may or may not mercifully realize that, after all, this is a great gain, because "God is not a *what*," not a "thing." That is precisely one of the essential characteristics of contemplative experience. It sees that there is no "what" that can be called God. There is "no such thing" as God because God is neither a "what" nor a "thing" but a pure "*Who*." He is the "Thou" before whom our inmost "I" springs into awareness. He is the I Am before whom with our own most personal voice we echo "I am."[5]

Thus Merton moves away from "what" language to personal pronouns. This move from what, or essence, to person is the basis for Walsh's rejection of the Boethian definition of person. In a footnote to the above, Merton stresses the experiential foundation for the preference for person language:

> This should not be taken to mean that man has no valid concept of the divine nature. Yet in contemplation abstract notions of the divine essence no longer play an important part since they are replaced by a concrete intuition, based on love of God as a *Person*, an object of love, not a "nature" or a "thing" which would be the object of study or of possessive desire.

Merton's reflections on person in God are thus guided by his experience in prayer. Though Walsh's conclusions are the same, he makes no such clear experiential claim. However, both Walsh and Merton see the person as a relationship with God rather than as a type of being.

From the Trinity issues the personal life, which is a life of mutual bestowal and presence in truth and love. "Love," Merton writes, "comes out of God and gathers us to God in order to pour itself back into God through all of us and bring us all back to Him on the tide of His own infinite mercy."[6] The human being, as God's image, has a capacity for this personal life; such is the human challenge and the divine invitation.

The origin of the person is located by Walsh within the Logos. Merton reflects this Logos Christology:

> It is the gift of God Who, in His mercy, completes the hidden and mysterious work of creation in us by enlightening our minds and hearts, by awakening in us the awareness that we are words spoken in His One Word.[7]

Human persons arise from within the Logos through God's creative love. As "words spoken in His One Word," human persons exemplify the Word. Merton does not use the term *imitability*, but the concept is implied in the phrase "words spoken in His One Word."

In addition to understanding persons as imaging God's own word, Merton also refers to finality. The notion of humans imaging God refers not only to origin but also to echoing God through human becoming. "We ourselves," Merton says, on p. 3 of *New Seeds*, "are words of His. But we are words that are meant to respond to Him, to answer Him, to echo Him. . . ."

The stress upon becoming expresses the dimension of vocation, or call,[8] to image God. Merton says that "our vocation is not simply to *be*, but to work together with God in the creation of our own life, our own identity, our own destiny."[9] Personhood involves transformation through fidelity to God's call. "The full Christian sense of the person," Merton writes, "is found in the recovery of our likeness to God, in Christ, by his Spirit."[10]

Though Merton, like Walsh, describes personhood in terms of imaging God, and finality through fidelity to call, he also gives attention to contingency. Unlike Walsh, Merton does not deny that the person is contingent. Merton links contingency with intuition of being and with the depth of one's identity:

> There exists some point at which I can meet God in a real and experimental contact with His infinite actuality. This is the "place" of God, His sanctuary — it is the point where my contingent being depends upon His love. Within myself is a metaphorical apex of existence at which I am held in being by my creator.[11]

Merton (*New Seeds*, p. 3) also describes contemplation as an awareness of one's contingency:

> Hence contemplation is a sudden gift of awareness, an awakening to the Real within all that is real. A vivid awareness of infinite Being at the roots of our own limited being. An awareness of our contingent reality as received as a present from God, as a free gift of love.

This experience of one's contingency and the implied intuition of divine love is an important element in Merton's description of human identity. Where Walsh does not see the person as contingent, Merton so profoundly values this dimension of personal identity that one would be distorting his thought to remove contingency and efficient causality as vital elements of the human person. Certainly all creatures are contingent, but only human persons can be conscious of their contingency.

Walsh's focus on the origin of the person within God does not include discussion of rebirth in Christ. Walsh, as noted in the previous chapter, wanted to highlight the original love of God in creation rather than in the work of redemption, which he did not deny. Merton explicitly acknowledges the necessity of supernatural elevation in order to be relating to God. "It is true," Merton says in *New Seeds of Contemplation*, "that God knows Himself in all the things that exist. He sees them, and it is because He sees them that they exist. . . . Insofar as He sees and loves them, all things reflect Him." Thus far Merton resonates with Walsh's idea of imitability, but Merton goes on to highlight the need for grace:

> But although God is present in all things by His knowledge and His love and His power and His care of them, He is not necessarily realized and known by them. He is only known and loved by those to whom He has freely given a share in His own knowledge and love of Himself. In order to know and love God as He is, we must have God dwelling in us in a new way, not only in His creative power but in His mercy. . . . God bridges the infinite distances between Himself and the spirits created to love Him, by supernatural missions of His own life. . . . My discovery of my identity begins and is perfected in these missions, because it is in them that God Himself, bearing in Himself the secret of who I am, begins to live in me not only as my creator but as my other and true self. (pp. 40-41)

Here Merton asserts the necessity of rebirth in Christ for the realization of one's true identity. It would be absurd, however, to imagine that he would deny the status of person to anyone who has not been born again or baptized. Persons emerge from God's creative love in the Logos and are guided to full participation in divine life through the indwelling Spirit, which, Merton emphasizes, is more than one's natural life.

Person versus Nature

THE NATURE-PERSON DISTINCTION that Walsh accepts and develops is also found in Merton's writings, in regard to both human and divine persons. The anthropological significance of the nature-person distinction in Merton is that *person* becomes a term for the human being that is beyond the body-soul distinction. Merton comments on this issue several years after *New Seeds* in his *Redeeming the Time*. "Christian anthropology," Merton writes, "is not yet fully clear about the person, since what belongs to the whole Christian person has traditionally been ascribed to the *soul* (part of the person only) and to grace."[12] As Walsh teaches, in harmony with medieval Christian thought, human nature consists of body and soul. Merton proceeds to distinguish person from human nature as body and soul:

> Let no one . . . dare to hate or to despise the body that has been entrusted to him by God. . . . Let him not desecrate his own natural unity by dividing himself, soul against body, as if the soul were good and the body evil. Soul and body together subsist in the reality of the hidden, inner person. If the two are separated from one another, there is no longer a person, there is no longer a living, subsisting reality made in the image and likeness of God. The "marriage" of body and soul in one person is one of the things that makes man the image of God. . . .
> It is equally false to treat the soul as if it were the "whole self" and the body as if it were the "whole self." Those who make the first mistake fall into the sin of angelism. Those who make the second live below the level assigned by God to human nature.[13]

Merton's teaching here combats any tendency to identify person with soul. Human nature as body and soul finds its unity in the person, in the self beneath the empirical ego. The unity of body and soul exhausts neither the depth of personhood nor the significance of person for Merton.

In addition to giving a term to prevent identification of person with any part of human nature, the spiritual significance of the nature-person distinction in Merton appears to be in his concern for experience of God versus relating to God as an abstract idea:

> In contemplation abstract notions of the divine essence no longer play an important part since they are replaced by a concrete intuition, based on love, of

God as a *Person*, an object of love, not a "nature" or a "thing" which would be the object of study or of possessive desire. (*New Seeds*, p. 13)

This concern for relationship emerges also in Merton's discussion, in the same work (p. 152), of contemplation and the humanity of Christ:

> No one can dismiss the Man Christ from his interior life on the pretext that he has now entered by higher contemplation into direct communication with the Word. For the Man Christ *is* the Word of God, even though His human nature is not His divine nature. . . .

Merton goes on, in *New Seeds*, to note that the Nestorian heresy involved a view of Christ and God as two beings rather than one being uniting two natures:

> The weakness of Nestorianism is that it equates the nature with the person. But Christian contemplation is supremely personalistic. Our love and knowledge of Christ do not terminate in His human *nature* or in His divine *nature* but in His *Person*. To love Him merely as a *nature* would be like loving a friend for his money or his conviviality. We do not love Christ for what He has but for *Who He is.*
>
> The "what" in Christ is vastly less important than the "Who." The "what" may or may not be imaginable, but we reach the "Who" — the mysterious ineffable Divine Person — *directly and immediately* through grace and love, without images (or *with* them if you like, but this is less direct) and without rationalization. The real mystery of Christian *agape* (charity) is this power that the Person of the Word, in coming to us, has given to us. The power of a direct and simple contact with Him, not as with an *object* only, a "thing" seen or imagined, but in the trans-subjective union of love which does not unite an object with a subject but *two subjects in one affective union.* (p. 153)

Thus *person* implies immediacy and directness, while *nature* implies abstraction and object knowledge. Merton, whose life was given to experience of God, uses person language in order to highlight a knowledge of God derived from encounter with God.

The nature-person distinction, when applied to human person and nature, implies the same preference for person encountered as a who over human nature as an abstract what. Merton expresses it this way: "It is not only human nature that is 'saved' by the divine mercy, but above all the human *person*" (p. 38).

The difference between person and nature reflects different epistemological levels: the level of experience, or encounter, versus the level of knowledge, or information. To encounter a person, human or divine, in love is not reducible to obtaining knowledge *about* that person, much less knowledge about what that person is.

As we will see in the chapter on unity, Merton applies the person-versus-nature distinction to the possibility of transcending nature. He speaks of the nature-oriented approach that treats human beings "as objects."[14] This understanding of nature corresponds to the object-centered consciousness just mentioned. Merton contrasts this nature-oriented approach with the person-oriented approach. The person-oriented approach does not try to control others as objects but rather responds to the freedom and intelligence in the other. The person-oriented approach believes that persons are not totally limited by natural necessity but can transcend nature.

Thus Merton's view of nature corresponds with Walsh's understanding. Nature in both is a principle of limit. The limits of human nature, such as a presumed aggressiveness, the person can transcend. If transcendence is merely a function of human freedom and intelligence, then one can say that the presumed limits of human nature can be transcended by an individual person's use of human nature. To be consistent with Merton's overall vision, one would also say that to transcend the limitations of an individual human nature, one would need to refer to one's relationship to God.

Like Walsh, Merton also speaks of nature as body and soul. Thus Merton's understanding of nature refers to the order of beings and to the beings within that order. Such an understanding is as traditional as Walsh's, which was pointed out in chapter III. The person is a unity underlying the type of being with its component coprinciples of body and soul.

Nature language in both Merton and Walsh refers to objects and abstract knowledge of objects, whereas person language pertains to intuitive immediacy in love. The nature is the what, while person is the who. The primary relationship of persons, as understood by both Merton and Walsh, is within God, then between God and humans, and, finally, between humans.

Person and Individual

PSYCHOLOGICALLY, THE INDIVIDUAL IS what is constructed by discrimination from all other individuals; the unique person is constituted by divine love. As Merton explains in *New Seeds of Contemplation*,

> People who know nothing of God and whose lives are centered on themselves, imagine that they can only find themselves by asserting their own desires and ambitions and appetites in a struggle with the rest of the world. They try to become real by imposing themselves on other people, by appropriating for themselves some share of the limited supply of created goods and thus emphasizing the difference between themselves and the other men who have less than they, or nothing at all.
>
> They can only conceive one way of becoming real: cutting themselves off from other people and building a barrier of contrast and distinction between themselves and other men. They do not know that reality is to be sought not in division but in unity, for we are "members of one another."
>
> The man who lives in division is not a person but only an individual.[15]

Identity founded on difference from all others is an identity founded on alienation. Here Merton's meaning of *individual* is as pejorative as Walsh's. Individuality is an insufficient basis for authentic existence, which derives from God's creative love, a love that all people share. The ascetical task, in Merton's view, is to save the person from the individual, to save what God has conceived from what humans in their selfish drive for security have fabricated (p. 38).

Merton, unlike Walsh, also speaks in positive terms of individuality in *New Seeds of Contemplation*. In a chapter titled "Things in their Identity," he asserts that things must be true to their individuality to be true to God:

> Each particular being, in its individuality, its concrete nature and entity, with all its own characteristics and its private qualities and its own inviolable identity, gives glory to God by being precisely what He wants it to be here and now, in the circumstances ordained for it by His Love and His infinite Art. (p. 30)

Not only are subhuman creatures to glorify God through their individuality, but also human beings. Merton writes (p. 31) that "it is true to say that for me sanctity consists in being myself and for you sanctity consists in being *your* self and that, in the last analysis, your sanctity will never be mine and mine will never be yours. . . ."

The positive note to individuality thus derives from God's will to create individuals, and Merton expresses the positive characteristics of individuality, in the last quotation, as incommunicability. Incommunicability is also a precious characteristic for Walsh, but Walsh reserves positive language to uniqueness rather than individuality. Merton, by ascribing both positive and negative connotations to "individuality," thus approximates ordinary English usage more than Walsh.

Merton's praise of individuality protects him from falling into the very abstractness he believes to be alien to contemplative knowledge of God. At the same time, Merton's pejorative meaning of individuality as self-created alienation is a key element in his analysis of the human condition. Like Walsh, though with less consistency, Merton uses the term *uniqueness* to describe the positive pole of human individuality.

Individuality and Uniqueness

AS NOTED ABOVE, the pejorative meaning of *individual* for Merton describes the human identity created by efforts to establish self in opposition to others rather than by living out God's establishment of oneself in His love. Lest the reader believe that individuality is contrary to God's creative will, Merton allows himself occasionally to speak in positive terms of individuality and also uses the term *uniqueness* to accompany his positive descriptions. Uniqueness reflects God's loving choice in creation. Merton writes that "it is not only human nature that is 'saved' by the divine mercy, but above all the human *person*. The object of salvation is that which is unique, irreplaceable, incommunicable — that which is myself alone" (p. 38).

This description of salvation of the person is salvation of the one God has in mind; anyone who tries to be someone else is trying to hide from God. Merton thus affirms the traditional Christian belief in continuity between one's earthly and heavenly selves. The logic of love demands that the otherness of the beloved not be swallowed up. Merton maintains immortality of individual persons rather than imagining them to be blended into one mass or so transcending their individual selves as no longer to exist.

Merton and Walsh could have saved their reader some confusion by noting that *individual* for them primarily has for them a psychological rather than metaphysical meaning. In effect, *uniqueness* is their term for metaphysical individuality, while *individuality*, especially when pejorative, refers to a particular consciousness or identity. To be identified totally with how one differs from others is to omit from one's identity one's divine origin, which all share.

Collectivity and Community

THE HUMAN PERSON EMERGES from the community called Trinity. That person is an image of divine love, which is originally communitarian. For Merton as well as for Walsh, community is the proper context for realization of personal love, while collectivity depersonalizes. The human capacity to love is affected by one's environment and perspective. In order to love in a godlike way, it helps to see oneself as related to God. Such a theological vision requires an ability to transcend what collective thinking has to say about human life; such transcendence, Merton writes, requires a measure of solitude:

> The need for true solitude is a complex and dangerous thing, but it is a real need. It is all the more real today when the collectivity tends more and more to swallow up the person in its shapeless and faceless mass. . . .
>
> True solitude is the home of the person, false solitude the refuge of the individualist. The person is constituted by a uniquely subsisting capacity to love — by a radical ability to care for all beings made by God and loved by Him. Such a capacity is destroyed by the loss of perspective. Without a certain element of solitude there can be no compassion because when a man is lost in the wheels of a social machine he is no longer aware of human needs as a matter of personal responsibility.[16]

(Note the Walshian concepts in this passage: person constituted by love; person contrasted with individualist; *collectivity* as a pejorative term for a human group.) Merton thus sees solitude as the context for the emergence of compassion, the emergence of genuine selfhood, or personhood. While solitude allows humans to transcend their isolated ego-centered existence, community helps them to express the love that is poured into their hearts. Merton contrasts living in communion with any collectivity that subordinates personal values to anything else.[17]

The source of Christian community is divine love and human awareness of that love. If Christians relate to each other solely in terms of personality traits rather than personhood, their relationships will not be words of God. To relate to others on the basis of personhood is to love Christ with the love of Christ. Ideally, such relationships will transcend personality differences to a level at which all are one in Him: the level of the mystical Christ who embraces all, "Jew and Greek, male and female."

With all of Merton's eloquent discussion of solitude and his championing of the eremitical life within the Cistercian Order, he is nevertheless insistent on the communal bond in charity that is the Church. His admission (*New Seeds*, p. 51) that he must find his identity, not only in God, but also in other people speaks of a realism that guards against false mysticism and false solitude. Although the Christian's deepest identity is found in a relationship with Christ, all human beings need the experience of human love if they are to be open to the depths of love manifested in Christ.

While physical solitude may cause isolation if it is not grounded in openness to God, Merton believes contemporary human beings are in danger of another type of isolation, the anonymous immersion into a faceless crowd, or collectivity. To be in a crowd, Merton says in *New Seeds*, may help a person to forget that he or she is alone, and such forgetfulness can deaden persons to their need for responsible communication with others.

> The collectivity tends more and more to swallow up the person in its shapeless and faceless mass. . . . Without a certain element of solitude there can be no compassion because when a man is lost in the wheels of a social machine he is no longer aware of human needs as a matter of personal responsibility.
> . . . The great temptation of modern man is not physical solitude but immersion in the mass of other men . . . escape into the great formless sea of irresponsibility which is the crowd. (pp. 53-54)

Collectivity deadens compassion and sensitivity to human

needs and swallows up human responsibility. Merton's hunger for justice, his interest in and involvement with such social issues at war, race, and violence draw on energy from his reverence for the person. It is in the collective anonymity of huge cities that the person is all too often lost.

In *The Nonviolent Alternative*, Merton expresses his belief that the attempt to deal with human problems by violence or coercion neglects persons in its efforts at dealing with humanity in general, which is nothing more than an abstraction:

> The violent or coercive approach to the solution of human problems considers man in general, in the abstract, and according to various notions about the laws that govern his nature. In other words, it is concerned with man as subject to necessity, and it seeks out the points at which his nature is consistently vulnerable in order to coerce him physically or psychologically.[18]

If the solution of human problems carries an awareness of persons, then their freedom must be respected. Nonviolence as a way of coping with dehumanization seeks to transcend the understanding of the human as merely governed by the inexorable laws of nature. The person is more than nature in that the person involves freedom and intelligence, which are irreducible. Nonviolence seeks to awaken others "to personal openness and to dialogue" (*The Nonviolent Alternative*, p. 217). The horror of war, the brutality of totalitarianism, the lifeless face of the city spring from forgetfulness of the personal. People become things, and love of things falls short of personal love.

To the oppressor, the collectivity is the convenient veil over personal worth. To the unawakened, the collectivity is protection from demands of truth, love, and responsibility.

True versus False Self

HOWEVER COMMITTED A PERSONALIST Merton is and however much he shares in Walsh's vocabulary, Merton's favorite expressions for dealing with the human person include language of self: true versus false self, or deep versus empirical self.[19] Although Walsh does not use these terms, the similarity of Merton's polarities to Walsh's insights are evident.

As Merton articulates Christian personalism, one's identity, one's personhood, is found in his or her relationship with God. A person is one who is called by God, one who is loved by God.[20] The discovery of one's true selfhood is the work of prayer; the simple awareness that one is loved by God is the door to Christian liberation. As in the following passage from *New Seeds of Contemplation*, Merton frequently contrasts transcendent, true, inner, or deep self with external and illusory self and empirical ego:

> There is an irreducible opposition between the deep transcendent self that awakens only in contemplation, and the superficial, external self which we commonly identify with the first person singular. We must remember that this superficial "I" is not our real self. It is our "individuality" and our "empirical self," but it is not truly the hidden and mysterious person in whom we subsist before the eyes of God. The "I" that works in the world, thinks about itself, is not the true "I" that has been united to God in Christ. It is at best the vesture, the mask, the disguise of that mysterious and unknown "self" whom most of us never discover until we are dead. Our external, superficial self is not eternal, not spiritual. Far from it. This self is doomed to disappear as completely as smoke from a chimney. It is utterly frail and evanescent. Contemplation is precisely the awareness that this "I" is really "not I" and the awakening of the unknown "I" that is beyond observation and reflection and is incapable of commenting upon itself. It cannot even say "I" with the assurance and the impertinence of the other one, for its very nature is to be hidden, unnamed, unidentified in the society where men talk about themselves and about one another. In such a world the true "I" remains both inarticulate and invisible, because it

has altogether too much to say — not one word of which is about itself.[21]

The process of liberation from the confusion of the external self involves a dying to all that is superficial, a dying to all false identifications. One's truest identity is as one loved by God. To awaken to one's personhood in the love of God is to grow in freedom from the need to affirm and assert oneself. One who is held in being by God need not frantically try to establish himself. One *is!* The self-denial intrinsic to asceticism is a denial of illusory selfhood.

Merton, by use of the language of deeper self, opens Christian personalism to mysticism. The "nights" of John of the Cross Merton interprets in terms of detachment from one's limited self. "The mystic lives in emptiness, and freedom, as if he had no longer a limited and exclusive 'self' that distinguished him from God and other men." This union with God, Merton recognizes, is a free gift from God, as is one's very existence; yet for the fullness of mystical union, one must "mean seriously to undertake a *total renunciation of all attachments*" (*New Seeds*, p. 210). Otherwise God will not free one from disunity and confusion.

Freedom from false identifications resonates with the ideal of the Upanishads, and freedom from the limited self points toward Zen. The "ecumenism" of Merton is a reflection of the process of purification found in mysticism, and mysticism is not confined to any particular religious tradition. While Merton is able to reach a depth that enables him to dialog with other traditions, he does so through his own Christian tradition. One's true identity, according to Eckhart — and Merton seems to agree — involves "the birth of Christ in us."[22] It is through the presence of Christ within oneself that one's true identity awakens.[23]

Merton dives into tradition, allowing the past to come alive in himself in order to reach the pearl of great price. In his sympathetic dialog with the Zen tradition, Merton does not denigrate Christian doctrine; rather, he sees doctrine as related to Christian experience.

True versus Cartesian Selfhood

IN HIS DEFENSE OF MYSTICISM against those who would reduce the mystical element in Christianity to Hellenistic accretion, Merton distinguishes selfhood that is in communion with God from Cartesian selfhood, which is enclosed in itself.[24]

Cartesian consciousness, for Merton, refers to the starting point for modern philosophy, in which the thinking subject is primary. Descartes' "I think, therefore I am" is, of course, a reversal of the Augustinian "I am, I know I am, and I love my being."[25] In Augustine, being precedes thinking. The Cartesian consciousness is caught up in observing self and developing self-awareness over against objects. The increase of such self-consciousness gives knowledge of how the objects relate to self, hence more control is given to the subject over these objects. Thus the thinking subject over against all else becomes capable of manipulating others.[26] Merton admits, in *Zen and the Birds of Appetite*, that such manipulation and control are important for those who are activists, as they must make many concrete decisions relative to the flux of their commitments (p. 29).

The image Merton offers for this Cartesian consciousness is a "solipsistic bubble":

> Modern man, insofar as he is still Cartesian . . . is a subject for whom his own self-awareness as a thinking, observing, measuring and estimating "self" is absolutely primary. It is for him the one indubitable "reality," and all truth starts here. The more he is able to develop his consciousness as a subject over against objects, the more he can understand things in their relations to him and one another, the more he can manipulate these objects for his own interests, but also, at the same time, the more he tends to isolate himself in his own subjective prison, to become a detached observer cut off from everything else in a kind of impenetrable alienated and transparent bubble which contains all reality in the form of purely subjective experience. Modern consciousness then tends to create this solipsistic bubble of aware-

ness — an ego-self imprisoned in its own consciousness, isolated and out of touch with other such selves insofar as they are all "things" rather than persons. (p. 22)

Instead of communion, one is left with detached observation in which other humans are reduced to objects. The heightening of the subject-object distinction in modern consciousness results in alienation and isolation. This form of alienation is symbolized by the situation in which one becomes an object to oneself (p. 24).

When Cartesian consciousness tries to relate to God, God becomes an *object* of consciousness. But since no one knows what God is, the Cartesian loses God. If God cannot be captured in a concept or located in a definite place, He does not fit into Cartesian consciousness.

In contrast to Cartesian consciousness, Merton speaks of an openness to being. He testifies to an experienced metaphysics, an intuition of being. The starting point is not self-consciousness but being, which is "beyond and prior to the subject/object division. Underlying the subjective experience of the individual self, there is an immediate experience of Being" (p. 23). The starting point is Being, which communicates being to each person and to all that is.

A way of clarifying such experience is to point to contingency: the recognition that one need not be but, nevertheless, is. Awareness of contingency is the underside of the awareness of being grounded in God's love, which holds all in being. To be in communion with the God of love, or the God who is self-diffusive goodness, is to be gifted with an openness to a reality that grounds one's own awareness (see *Zen*, pp. 23-25). Openness characterizes this awareness of Being, whereas "over against" characterizes Cartesian consciousness.

The true self is centered on God, not on itself. The true self encounters God in its own freedom and love, not as an object. Relative to God, "empirical self is seen by comparison to be nothing; that is to say, contingent, evanescent, relatively real, real only in relation to its source and end in God . . ." (p. 26). The "nothingness" of the empirical self needs elaboration, although in the above quotation Merton gives qualifications that would satisfy the demands of the most orthodox.

Though Merton defends contemplative consciousness and its traditional metaphysical intuition and language against self-reflective Cartesian consciousness, he does admit the possibility that classical metaphysical language may not be accessible to modern minds. Even with help from Zen and yoga, he allows that such language may be worn out. In an attempt to acknowledge the possibility of superseding classical metaphysical language, Merton offers elements of future approaches to self corresponding to needs that must be met.

The first need, the need for community, reflects Merton's awareness that self-development requires communication in knowledge and love with other human beings (p. 30). The second need is for an understanding of one's everyday self in ordinary life. Here Merton says that the idealistic philosophers tend to lead their followers to celestial realms. He does not accuse classical metaphysics of this otherworldly focus but says that the outlook of classical metaphysics, "in proportion as it was *idealistic* . . . did tend to misconstrue and depreciate the concrete" (ibid.).

There is no ground for interpreting those words of Merton as an intended criticism of Walsh, but they may be applied to Walsh as a qualification. I have observed students showing discontent at Walsh's "idealistic" presentation of self. After all, Walsh uses preexistence and heavenly perfection as the paradigmatic situations of true personhood. That Merton does not depreciate the concrete and the ordinary is an advance over Walsh's descriptions.

Merton also stresses the need for an integral rather than a partial experience of self. By his use of the term *integral*, Merton includes all levels: body, mind, emotions, imagination, spirit. He does not advocate focusing on one part of the whole. This third need suggests that Merton would deny the identification of true self with soul, or "*apex mentis*," in opposition to mere emotions or Brother Ass. "True self" means self in relation to God. Merton is careful, more careful than Walsh, to affirm individual as well as personal reality:

The fulfillment of our destiny is not merely to be lost in God, as the traditional figures of speech would have it, like a drop of water in a barrel of wine or like iron in the fire, but *found* in God in all our individual and personal reality.[27]

Merton also emphasizes a fourth need, the need of modern people to be free from "inordinate self-consciousness" and from "obsession with self-affirmation" in order to enjoy simply being oneself.[28] This need finds expression throughout Merton's writings, and one may assume this burden of inordinate self-awareness and concern is shared by Merton himself, who sets as a goal to become lost to oneself.[29]

The empirical ego, or superficial self, is not, for Merton, merely the pleasure seeker. As the monastic tradition has noted, the spiritual seeker who has attained some freedom from gluttony, avarice, lust, acedia, and envy is then likely to be overcome by vainglory and pride.[30] In other words, the very project of seeking God, or transcendence, can isolate the self from communion.[31] One of the particular dangers of the solitary life is becoming caught up in oneself without allowing the needs of others to touch one very deeply. Solitaries can become experts of their own journey and become very concerned with their own progress or state of soul. This type of self-concern fits Merton's description of Cartesian ego-consciousness. "I think, therefore I am" can be unconsciously translated by the inflated self-image of the professional God seeker into "I have experienced, therefore, I am."[32] Such a seeker is leaving behind mere thinking, which characterizes ordinary consciousness; such a seeker is pushing into the "great beyond," where, by association, the seeker becomes great!

When one begins to seek mystical experience and to accumulate such experiences, Merton doubts if any real transcendence occurs. Such a reflexively self-concerned consciousness, Merton writes in *Zen and the Birds of Appetite*, is an obstacle to genuine transcendence:

> In all these higher religious traditions the path to transcendence realization is a path of ascetic self-

emptying and "self-naughting" and not at all a path of self-affirmation, of self-fulfillment, or of "perfect attainment." That is why it is felt necessary by these traditions to speak in strong negative terms about what happens to the ego-subject, which instead of being "realized" in its own limited selfhood is spoken of rather as simply vanishing out of the picture altogether. The reason for this is not that the person loses his metaphysical or even physical status, or regresses into non-identity, but rather that his *real* status is quite other than what appears empirically to us to be his status. Hence it becomes overwhelmingly important for us *to become detached from our everyday conception of ourselves as potential subjects for special and unique experiences, or as candidates for realization, attainment and fulfillment.* (p. 76)

To let go of attachment to self-identity derived from what one can achieve or from the approval of others does not mean regression into a state of nonidentity or into some sort of Freudian "oceanic swoon" (p. 72). Rather, one lets go of illusion to be more truly who he or she is. Since God is ungraspable, the religiously intense may try to grasp religious experience in the hope of establishing self as "spiritual" or special in some way.

Merton's advice to one attempting to make progress is "to relax his grasp on his concept of what that goal is and 'who it is' that will attain it. To cling too tenaciously to the 'self' and its own fulfillment would guarantee that there would be no fulfillment at all" (p. 77). For transcendent experience not to be falsified, the experiencing subject has to, as it were, disappear (p. 76).

The subject-object mode of relating, Merton believes, is inadequate to interpersonal love. To love another as object is to love the other as a thing, which is hardly love. Genuine interpersonal love "communes in the subjectivity of the one loved." This is knowledge by identity. Such identification with the other does not do away with or violate the subjectivity of the other. Instead, genuine interpersonal love "transforms us so to speak into the other person, making us able to see things as he sees them, love what he loves, experience the deeper realities of his own life as if they were our own."[33] Such transformation requires sacrifice of selfishness and opens the way to relating to God, not as a thing, but as loving Father.

Prayer

TO DEMONSTRATE THE EQUIVALENCE in meaning of person in Walsh and Merton, it has been convenient to reproduce a number of the same topics from the preceeding chapter on Walsh. In that chapter, Walsh's personalistic thought was held up as providing a basis for spirituality. Most of Merton's writings, unlike Walsh's, directly pertain to elements of spiritual life. While prayer is only implicitly dealt with in Walsh's thought, Merton devotes volumes to prayer.

Through the awareness of the love of God, one is enabled to let go of the self-centered quest for security. Through awareness of being loved and held in being, a person is able to loosen his or her tight control on life. In Calcutta shortly before his death, Thomas Merton pointed to true selfhood and to its prayerful and communal realization:

> Who am I? My deepest realization of who I am is — I am one loved by Christ. This is a very important conception. It takes us below the mere level where I decide who I am by the reaction of persons to me. On the social level we create identities for one another by the way we treat each other. If you treat a sister as a difficult person you make her a difficult person. . . . Expectations of other people are secondary. . . . The depth of our identity is in the center of my being where I am known by God. I know He sees me: I am glad He sees me and His seeing is love and mercy and acceptance. The great central thing in Christian Faith and Hope is the courage to realize oneself and to accept oneself as loved by God even though one is not worthy. Identity does not consist in creating

worthiness, because He loves us in any way. We know God loves us as we are.[34]

One's identity at its deepest level is one loved by God. If one is able to accept God's love, one is thereby liberated from ego's desperate attempts to assert itself. Furthermore, the human sense of unworthiness is dwarfed by God's mercy. One's deepest identity is hidden in His merciful love. From such grateful freedom arises the possibility of loving others in Christ.

Freedom

FREEDOM AND PERSONHOOD, or identity, are linked at a couple of points in Merton's thought. Above, in the discussion of collectivity, we saw Merton's concern for the modern human being's temptation to escape from freedom and personal responsibility by hiding within a faceless crowd or within the mass mind. Merton describes the essential role of freedom in shaping one's identity:

> Our vocation is not simply to *be*, but to work together with God in the creation of our own life, our own identity, our own destiny. We are free beings and sons of God. This means to say that we should not passively exist, but actively participate in His creative freedom, in our own lives, and in the lives of others, by choosing the truth. To put it better, we are even called to share with God the work of *creating* the truth of our identity.[35]

These words on freedom come from a man who spent more than a quarter of a century under a rule and an abbot. Freedom, as Merton writes in *New Seeds of Contemplation*, means "the ability to do the will of God" (p. 201). The struggle with illusion requires a lifelong relationship with God in order to bring about His vision and intention. Merton says, in the same work, that *"the seeds that are planted in my liberty at every moment, by God's will, are the seeds of my own reality, my own happiness, my own sanctity."* (p. 33). Unlike Walsh,

Merton placed himself under a monastic regimen that demanded endless subjugations of his will. Merton learned freedom through a rigorous school of obedience. Considering the price he paid, it is no wonder that freedom is intimately connected with his understanding of the way of personal realization.

Merton emphasizes human freedom to the point of seeing it as a component of the human person. While commenting on "The Constitution of the Church in the Modern World," from the Second Vatican Council, Merton, echoing themes found in Walsh, calls for a renewed Christian personalism:

> The true focus of Christian humanism is not human *nature* but the human *person*. In fact, it is because he is a person that man has the freedom to transcend his nature and to master its demands, using the natural powers he has received, not simply in order to fulfill the purposes of nature itself (the good of the species or of the collectivity) but personal and spiritual emancipation for himself and others. The person is more than the ego (the individual nature). It is not man's ego that makes him capable of "likeness to God," but his personal freedom to respond to life and to love beyond the limited requirements of the ego. This is especially true in relations with the other person.[36]

Here freedom is the likeness to God, and Merton speaks of a freedom to transcend "the purposes of nature" which include "the good of the species." These thoughts echo Walsh's earlier reflections (quoted in the preceding chapter):

> For individual substances of nonrational and nonintellectual nature exist for the precise ends of the species of which they are members. Spiritual creatures as persons are created for God and for themselves.[37]

Merton points to human freedom as the faculty that enables the human person to rise above "the good of the species." As noted above, he sees freedom as "the ability to do the will of God." Thus Merton and Walsh help the reader to focus on the human person, who reflects relationship with God in freedom. Merton is addressing a naturally human-centered audience. He does not dismiss humanism but tries to protect Christian humanism from reducing its understanding of human beings as likeness to God to a self-enclosed reality. During Merton's century theoreticians have attempted to limit the human to sexuality, aggression, or power. Merton, in common with Walsh, sees the human person as endowed with a freedom that can ratify the relationship with God and image God's relationship with creation.

Concluding Remarks

MERTON'S THOUGHT ABOUT THE TRUE SELF, or the person, is basically the same as that of Walsh, as shown above, especially in the person-nature distinction. Nature refers to what one is, whereas who one is derives from relationship with God. Persons are images of God. One benefits from examining Merton's use of the word *person* in order to appreciate the Trinitarian backdrop for his understanding of selfhood. Merton prefers the language of true, or deep, self versus empirical ego when discussing what Walsh calls "person." Through the language of self and identity, Merton is more experiential than Walsh.

While Merton, like Walsh, includes the ideas of image of God, or exemplarity, and finality in his understanding of person, he maintains that contingency is an important dimension of human existence. Merton further understands awareness of contingency to be a form of contemplation. That Merton emphasizes the importance of contingency and intuition of one's being as originating from God's love suggests that he would not separate contingency, or efficient causality, from finality and exemplarity.

That Walsh can separate contingency from the meaning of person helps to explain why his thought on the person is less concrete than Merton's. Merton also gives greater emphasis to freedom than does Walsh.

Walsh's treatment of person easily leads to an interpretation that denigrates individuality. Merton, on the other hand, maintains the therapeutic pointing beyond empirical ego to deeper self, and he also is careful to assert that individuality is not to be swallowed up or dissolved.

Both Merton and Walsh look to person as a key notion for spiritual living. They see prayer as a path toward awakening to the level of person, or the true self. Merton develops the social implications of personalist consciousness more than Walsh, but both see the insight into self, or person, as the necessary basis for a loving community.

As Walsh does not use the term "true versus empirical self," the link between Merton and Walsh is the word *person*. While *person* has great theological resonance, the language of self is immediately experiential.

NOTES FOR CHAPTER IV

1. Walsh, "Theology of Mysticism," group discussion, Abbey of Gethsemani, May 8, 1975; p. 3.
2. Walsh, "Person and Community I," pp. 6-7; "Some Intimations," p. 2.
3. For self as image of God, see *NM*, pp. 51-68; for issues of identity and identity crisis, see *CWA*, chapters 1-3; *LL*, sections I and III. Merton treats the exterior self in detail in *CP*, pp. 96-102, and in *IE*, especially pp. 3-56. Merton's social concerns as person-centered emerge clearly in his *The Nonviolent Alternative* (New York: Farrar, Straus & Giroux, 1980) especially pp. 63-66 and 208-218 (hereafter cited as *NVA*).
4. For treatments of Merton's teaching on self without reference to Walsh, see Higgins, pp. 58-63, and Malits, pp. 127-138.
5. *NS*, p. 3.
6. Ibid., p. 67; also Merton, *Seeds of Contemplation* (New York: New Directions, 1949), p. 50 (hereafter cited as *SC*).
7. *NS*, pp. 4-5.
8. Merton also writes of call in *CMP*; reprinted as *CP*, p. 68: "My true identity lies hidden in God's call to my freedom and my response to him." In *CWA*, pp. 220-221, Merton speaks mainly of the call to become "the person one is truly meant to be."
9. *NS*, p. 32.
10. *LL*, p. 203.
11. *NS*, p. 37.
12. Merton, *Redeeming the Time* (London: Burns & Oates, 1966), p. 56.
13. *NS*, p. 27.
14. *NVA*, p. 217.
15. *NS*, pp. 47-48.
16. Ibid., p. 53; for a similar use of the word *collective*, see Merton, *Raids on the Unspeakable* (New York: New Directions, 1966), pp. 15-17, and Merton's *CGB*, p. 97, where Merton links *collective* with *illusion*.
17. *NS*, p. 59.
18. *NVA*, p. 216.
19. A clear indication of Merton's identification of "true self" with person occurs in *ZBA*, p. 128, where he distinguishes true self from false self: "It is not the true self, the Christian person, the image of God stamped with the likeness of Christ."
20. Merton, "A Conference on Prayer, Calcutta, October 27, 1968," *Sisters Today*, no. 41 (April 1970), p. 452.
21. *NS*, pp. 7-8.

22. *ZBA*, pp. 39, 45, 56.
23. *NS*, p. 42.
24. *ZBA*, pp. 17-25.
25. Augustine, *City of God* (New York: The Modern Library, 1950), 11.26.
26. *ZBA*, p. 22.
27. Merton, *Last of the Fathers* (New York: Harcourt Brace, 1954), p. 52.
28. *ZBA*, p. 31.
29. *SSM*, pp. 309, 318, 322; *SJ*, pp. 18, 35; *ZBA*, p. 78; *Collected Poems*, pp. 452, 893; *LL*, p. 19.
30. John Cassian, *Conferences*, 5.10.
31. See "Gelasseheit" in Merton's *Collected Poems*, p. 452.
32. *ZBA*, p. 73.
33. Merton, "Love and Person," *Sponsa Regis*, no. 32 (September 1960), pp. 6-7.
34. Merton, "A Conference on Prayer, Calcutta, October 1968," pp. 452-453.
35. *NS*, p. 32.
36. Merton, *Redeeming the Time*, p. 56.
37. Walsh, "Some Reflections on the Concept of Substance in Medieval Philosophy," p. 104.

V

THE KEY TO MERTON'S THOUGHT

INTEREST IN MERTON IS WIDESPREAD and diverse. There are those within Christianity who are interested in prayer, attracted to Merton the spiritual writer; those whose religion largely consists in the thirst for justice, attracted to Merton the social critic; and those seekers of God whose lives have been touched by Eastern mysticism, attracted to Merton the Orientalist. This book deals most directly with Merton the spiritual writer, but other Mertons need comment. As Merton searched throughout his adult life for unity, the notion of several Mertons seems incongruous.

This chapter focuses on the unity in Merton, the continuity of his concerns. Social criticism was an interest throughout his adult life, as was Oriental spirituality. In addition to this unity on the level of interest is the unity of insight beneath the variety of social issues and Oriental teachings that Merton discusses. That underlying point of reference is the person. Merton seeks for principles of intelligent dialog on social issues *and* Oriental spirituality. His principles for such dialog reveal his underlying concern with the person. As we have seen in earlier chapters, being in relationship with God is the core meaning of personhood; that is, the origin, way, and end of life is one's relationship with God.

In the thirties, a philosopher named Stephen C. Pepper

wrote of "root metaphor" in philosophical discourse. A root metaphor is a hypothesis about the world or reality based on "a rather small set of facts and then explained in reference so as to cover all facts."[1] The root metaphor for Merton as well as for Walsh is the person. The person, for Merton, is the source of reality, the goal of reality, the highest value for human existence. Merton's social criticism and Oriental interest, if viewed from the optic of the person, are expressions of a unified apprehension of reality or, minimally, in Pepper's terms, expressions of his world hypothesis.

This underlying unity of the several Mertons is not always grasped. One of the recent commentators on Merton, Monica Furlong, illustrates how a reader may fail to see the unity relative to Merton's interest in social issues. Furlong's work *Merton: A Biography* creatively pieces together a picture of Merton's life through heavy reliance upon his correspondence.[2] However successful she has been in bringing forth the drama of this complex figure in American Christianity, she occasionally errs by oversimplifying Merton's development.

Continuity of Concern

DETAILS AND DIRECTION OF MERTON'S LIFE are familiar to his readers from his autobiographical writings. The "turn to the world" is a commonly acknowledged part of his development.[3] If care is not given to describing that turn, understanding of the continuity in Merton's life may be lost. Furlong writes of a change in Merton "that had turned him outward facing the problems of the world instead of inward to the concerns of the monastery."[4] The error is in the word *instead*.

Indisputably, Merton attended to issues of race, war and peace, environment, technology, and human culture in general. His anthropological interests extended from South Pacific Islanders to American Indians. The widening of Merton's horizon, however, did not mean that he turned away from the concerns of the monastery. A perusal of Merton's literary output in the 1960s should dispel the opinion that his interest in social issues was *instead* of his interest in monastic issues.

On opening Breit's *Thomas Merton: A Bibliography* at random, one finds a plethora of monastic articles written in the sixties. On pages 24-26, for example, are listed articles and book reviews on *Acedia*, on *Conversatio Morum*, on the topic of virginity, and on such monastic writers as the English mystics and Theophane the Recluse. These articles come out of the same period during which Furlong asserts that Merton had turned away from concern with the monastery.

Until his death, Merton wrote about monastic themes in an effort to facilitate renewal of monastic life. Rather than seeing his turn toward social issues as a turn away from concern with the monastery, a more accurate view would account for the interior unity linking monastery and world in Merton's heart.

Elena Malits has clearly charted Merton's movement from world rejection to compassion.[5] This movement implies, not rejection of interiority, but a deepening of interiority based on self-knowledge that enabled Merton to recognize that he is in the same condition as everyone else. This insight harmonizes with the emphasis on self-knowledge, which, as was shown earlier, is so much a part of his Cistercian tradition and his general vision of Christian life. In 1941, Merton reflected upon his attitude toward war expressed in his novel, *My Argument with the Gestapo:*

> The false solution went like this: the whole world, of which the war is a characteristic expression, is evil. It has therefore to be first ridiculed, then spat upon, and at last formally rejected with a curse.[6]

Merton's hindsight is harsh, for in his novel he acknowledges that "if anything happens to the world, it is partly because of me."[7] He did not know clearly what was to be his total response to the evil in society, but he had enough clarity to know that he needed to begin with the evil in his own heart.

Merton grows, not only from self-knowledge, but also from interaction with others, particularly through his years of teaching and directing others in the monastery.[8] Through listening to the troubles of his young students, Merton enters what he calls his new desert, compassion.[9]

Methodological Development

FROM EARLY ADULTHOOD to the end of his life, Merton engaged in social criticism. In addition to this unity of concern over social issues, one finds a unity in Merton's use of principles in his social criticism. He moves from random social criticism to the employment of theological principles by which he evaluates and gives perspective to social realities. A further unifying note attaches to these principles: they are expressions of Merton's underlying insight into and concern for the person.

Merton's work *The Secular Journal* presents criticism in nearly every entry, much of it social criticism. The variety of topics, from "ice-cold English spite" to "bourgeois prejudices" to American commercialization of Mother's Day, defies complete categorization. One would expect that a more mature Merton would reflect a more unified understanding of social issues and world events. Such unified understanding emerges, but he is realistic enough in *Conjectures of a Guilty Bystander* to admit the irreducibility of history to metaphysical categories:

> If at every instant one feels bound to grasp the entire and absolute truth supposedly underlying a concrete and contingent series of acts, and if his political life is nothing but a series of absolute judgments of right and wrong, determined, from moment to moment, for all eternity: this is an insane way to exist.
>
> The first thing one must learn to accept, indeed to choose, is the evident impossibility of giving everything a clear, definitive meaning. (pp. 191-192)

In the same book (pp. 203-207), Merton praises the thought of Thomas Aquinas, evidence that his respect for the historical does not exclude a philosophy or theology that attempts to be synthetic. Merton points to the focus upon the concrete, which is Aristotle's gift to Christian thought, especially in St. Thomas. In addition, Merton contrasts the thought of Thomas with the "apocalyptic enthusiasm" of Joachim of Flora and his followers. The latter, in Merton's opinion, unable to deal constructively with change, turned away from the world to the end. Thomas, on the other hand, turns to the world and to "the possibilities the world had in itself" (pp. 207-208). Again, Merton insists on an element of unknowing when turning to the world.

> You do not need to know precisely what is happening or exactly where it is all going. What you need is to recognize the possibilities and challenges offered by the present moment, and to embrace them with courage, faith, and hope. In such an event, courage is the authentic form taken by love. (p. 208)

Thus we find in Merton a respect for the historical as well as an appreciation of the synthetic and the metaphysical.

The salutary response to the crises of the sixties includes a quest for unity, but that quest is not a preoccupation with inner unity. Rather the quest is in terms of union with other people (p. 209), which we recognize as historical experience. Merton reveals his source for this conclusion by recalling how profoundly affected he has been by his interaction with those novices and students given to him for formation:

> It has been a great gift of His love to me, that I am their Novice Master. It is very good to have loved these people and been loved by them....
> From this basic experience one can, after all, recover hope for the other dimension of man's life: the political. Even though we have the power to destroy the whole world, life is stronger than the death instinct and love is stronger than hate. (p. 214)

As Merton wrestles with the world, his hope rests in the personal.

The historical experience of the love of and for his novices he links with the Incarnation and the doctrine of the Mystical Body, and on the basis of that linkage he has hopes for world peace:

> Because there is love in the world, and because Christ

> has taken our nature to Himself, there remains always the hope that man will finally, after many mistakes and even disasters, learn to disarm and to make peace recognizing that he *must* live at peace with his brother. (ibid.)

This linkage of historical experience and theological principle thus enables Merton to generalize about the future of society. However questionable the argument that the love of a small group of novices conjoined with the love of God in Christ leads to hope for world peace, we can at least see Merton's implicit methodology.

The linkage of interpersonal love between members of a religious community and the love of God embracing human nature in Christ also reflects the personalistic framework of Merton. God's interpersonal life leads to Incarnation, and that life is also operating in the bonds between members of His Mystical Body.

A few pages after the above reflections about his love for the novices, Merton, in *Conjectures*, deepens his thinking about the world with discussion of the intuition of being. Merton uses this word *being* in such a way that God's interpersonal love shines through:

> The doctrine of creation is rooted not in a desperate religious attempt to account for the fact that the world exists . . . the doctrine of creation . . . starts not from a *question about being* but from a *direct intuition of the act of being.*
>
> Such an intuition is simply an immediate grasp of one's own inexplicable personal reality in one's own incommunicable act of existing!
>
> One who has experienced the baffling, humbling, and liberating clarity of this immediate sense of what it means to be has in that very act experienced something of the presence of God. For God is present to me in the act of my own being, an act which proceeds directly from His will and is His gift. My act of being is a direct participation in the Being of God. (pp. 220-221)

By focusing on intuition of being, the interpersonal love that Merton experiences in the monastery as formation director is integrated into his theological experience of all reality grounded in personal love. Through this intuition, Merton sees his own being and that of all others as participations in God's act of existence. Without such a basis for respect, activity designed to transform the world leads to "destruction and abasement" (p. 222).

Throughout Merton's writings on social issues, one feels — behind the particulars of the issue — his commitment to the person. Turning from the journals of Merton to his treatises on topics relating to peace, the reader detects in Merton a more self-consciously rigorous foundation than in his journals. Again his employment of theological principles does not lead to answers for all questions; Merton uses principles that are linked to his intuition of the person.

In his 1964 essay "The Christian in World Crisis," Merton reflects upon Pope John XXIII's encyclical *Pacem in Terris* and on the general "moral climate" of the sixties.[10] Merton grounds Christian social obligation in the repercussions of the Incarnation, saying, on p. 21, "If God has become man, then no Christian is ever allowed to be indifferent to man's fate." Since God in Christ has embraced human nature, all people deserve to be "regarded as Christ. For all are at least potentially members of the Mystical Christ" (ibid.).

These theological foundation stones of the Incarnation and Mystical Body Merton lays as bases for arousing the moral conscience of Christians uncertain of their duty toward a world in crisis. With these theological foundations in mind, Merton turns to *Pacem in Terris* and focuses upon equivalent principles in that encyclical: "The greater part of the encyclical concentrates on basic principles: the dignity of the human person and the primacy of the universal common good over the particular good of the political unit" (p. 23).

In light of these principles, Merton criticizes an opinion of certain Christians that accepts a caricature of particular nations as evil. Such an opinion, he judges, would justify a first-strike mentality (p. 26). Note that this criticism is in light of theological principles that express Merton's personalism.

This principled criticism is an advance in method over the random approach of *The Secular Journal*.

Later, in "The Christian in World Crisis," Merton asks about the traditional attitude of the Christian peacemaker (p. 35). Before dealing with that attitude, Merton restates the same theological principles invoked fifteen pages earlier — the Incarnation and the Mystical Body — and the obligations toward all other people that flow from these principles.

The development sketched above is in terms of Merton's transition from undisciplined criticism to theologically principled criticism in service of an underlying concern for the person. Another example will show more clearly that Merton's social comment is rooted in an intuition of the person that remains true to Walsh's intuition, even though Walsh did not directly write about social issues.

"Blessed are the Meek: The Christian Roots of Nonviolence" was written late in Merton's life.[11] After an introduction that disposes of false understandings of nonviolence, Merton begins to look for principles:

> Christian nonviolence is not built on a presupposed division, but on the basic unity of man. It is not out for the conversion of the wicked to the ideas of the good, but for the healing and reconciliation of man with himself, man the person and man the human family.[12]

Merton's foundation for Christian nonviolence is human unity based upon the human person, and the person as part of the human family. These concepts are synonymous with the terms of the earlier article mentioned above: "the dignity of the human person" and the common good.

Merton defers to Gandhi's recognition that "the fully consistent practice of nonviolence demands a solid metaphysical and religious basis both in being and in God" (ibid.). Here Merton's call for a metaphysical foundation for social action is explicit. He points to the universal salvific will of God as a Christian basis, that is — *all* people are called to the kingdom of God. Who then can be treated as mere enemy?

Nonviolent methods are more in harmony with Merton's personalism than violent methods. Merton gives conditions for true nonviolence, and these reveal his concern for the person. Nonviolence is to be dedicated to truth, not just to truth for one's own group (pp. 209, 212). Truth for Merton is metaphysical, and through our prior examination of Walsh, we know that at the heart of being is personal love. Merton stresses the efficacy of love over power, for power serves special interests. Love, on the other hand, is committed to the good of everyone. Love seeks to dialog (p. 213). A dialog committed to truth allows its participants to learn even from "the adversary" (p. 214). The dialogical attitude of the nonviolent assumes a trust in the goodness of others (p. 215). Why else listen?

The violent approach is contrasted with the nonviolent in such a way as to bring out their respective views of the human being. In this contrast, Merton uses the nature-person distinction. The approach of violence, or coercion, rests on the human being as subject to the real or imagined laws of human nature. "It is concerned," says Merton, "with man as subject to necessity, and it seeks out the points at which his nature is consistently vulnerable in order to coerce him physically or psychologically" (p. 216).

In "Blessed are the Meek," Merton does not specify what these laws of human nature are that imprison humans in a deterministic world, but one may find those specifics elsewhere in his writings on social issues. For example, Merton writes of those, including Konrad Lorenz, author of *On Aggression*, and Robert Ardrey, author of *African Genesis*, as well as Nazi ideologues, all of whom believe in man's inborn aggressive tendency (pp. 196, 197, 168-171). Merton suggests that the American military draft system existed on the obsessive fear of the destructive aggression and hostility in the communist enemy (p. 197).

The nature-oriented approach manipulates human beings "as objects." The person-oriented mind "does not seek so much to *control* as to *respond*, and to *awaken response*" (p. 217). The person-oriented approach seeks dialog through free exercise of reason and love. The person-oriented mind believes that human beings are now slaves to laws of aggression and fear but, rather, have the capacity "to transcend nature and natural necessity" (ibid.).

Human nature, whether described as "aggressive" by Lorenz or "rational" by Aristotle, does not exhaust the meaning of a human being. The person is the hope of the human; the person, however determined, can take up a position toward his or her conditioning. The person can rethink and forgive, can give and take, can awaken a supposed enemy to a truth that both may serve. The way of violence trusts in weapons because human beings are not seen as worthy of trust. The person can transcend fear through faith and hope in the call of love, the call of God operating in the adversary. The way of nonviolence is the political face of person-centered living.[13]

I would like to discuss a key passage from Merton's most socially conscious journal, *Conjectures of a Guilty Bystander*, in such a way as to illustrate that his underlying insight into the person guides his social comment.

> The doctrine of creation is rooted not in a desperate religious attempt to account for the fact that the world exists . . . the doctrine of creation . . . starts not from a *question about being* but from a *direct intuition of the act of being.*
>
> Such an intuition is simply an immediate grasp of one's own inexplicable personal reality in one's own incommunicable act of existing!
>
> One who has experienced the baffling, humbling, and liberating clarity of this immediate sense of what it means to *be* has in that very act experienced something of the presence of God. For God is present to me in the act of my own being, an act which proceeds directly from His will and is His gift. My act of being is a direct participation in the Being of God. (pp. 220-221)

The first point of reference is, in Merton's words, "intuition of the act of being," which phrase evokes the work of Jacques Maritain, especially his *Preface to Metaphysics*, which was recommended by students of Walsh to the monks of Gethsemani. The neo-Thomist Maritain's understanding of intuition of being includes what Merton describes as "an immediate grasp of one's own inexplicable personal reality in one's own incommunicable act of existing!" For Merton, intuition of being is a grasp of the act of existing, including one's own. In the thirties, Maritain wrote, of the same experience of being, that "there is a kind of sudden intuition which a soul may receive of her own existence, or of 'being' embodied in all things whatsoever, however lowly."[14]

The second point that emerges from the quotation of Merton on intuition of being is that the intuition of one's own being implies God: "This immediate sense of what it means to *be* has in that very act experienced something of the presence of God."[15] Here again Merton does not explain beyond giving brief reference to "participation in the Being of God" two sentences later.

I feel safe in explaining the connection between intuition of his own being and awareness of God in terms of contingency. Merton approvingly quotes Maritain's remark about the intuition of being: "I have often experienced in a sudden intuition the reality of my being, the profound first principle which makes me exist outside nonentity" (p. 222). To awaken to one's being is to awaken to one's divine source.

The obscuring of personhood, or of relationship with God, is the danger that Merton identifies with life in technological society. Human fallenness Merton describes in terms of illusory identity in which a person ignores his or her relationship with God and falls into exteriority. Exteriority is the pursuit of happiness in things apart from one's origin and end in divine love. Life in technological society helps to veil one's true origin and end by providing an identity defined in relationship to the production system.

In *Conjectures of a Guilty Bystander*, Merton analyzes the moral dangers of technological society. He believes that people are living under the illusion that "mechanical progress means human improvement." The identification of this illusion is not original with Merton, who acknowledges Lewis Mumford as its source.[16] Merton's creative contribution resides in the more characteristically contemplative insight that sees this faith in technological progress to be a subplot in the more primal story of complete moral autonomy, which in turn is symptomatic of an ignorance of being, of being a gift, of being a person in the Walshian sense." The real root-sin of modern man," Merton writes in *Conjectures*, "is that in ignoring and condemning being and especially his own being, he has made his existence a disease and an affliction" (p. 221, 226).

What is more obvious than the fact that one is? Though nobody can consciously deny his own existence, the way people live tends to deny what is rationally undeniable. As persons develop, they collect information about who they think they are. People show how uncertain they are of their own existence by a nearly lifelong series of demands: "Listen to me!" "Watch me!" These childish pleas are carried into adulthood, at which time they are politely refined into efforts to receive attention and approval from others.

A person spends school years trying to survive both academically and socially. This survival project is not a matter of biology; physical survival is relatively easy in modern society. Social survival or academic survival, on the other hand, may require all of a person's cunning. What does such survival mean? To survive socially means to be held in sufficient esteem by other people that they affirm one's existence. Such survival consists in being in the minds of others.

The striving for approval, the striving to establish oneself in the minds of others, involves metaphysical ignorance, or, as Merton writes, ignorance of one's own being. This ignorance is in paradoxical tension with the fact that people will readily admit that they exist. Yet in practice many of these same people spend much of their energy trying to establish themselves. If persons are mindful of their being, how can they engage in activities designed to establish themselves?

Clearly a person's development and survival require recognition and support from others. These others enable one to love and come to a sense of self. But people come and go, forget one another and are forgotten; yet a person is not dissolved by the fading away of thoughts in the minds of others. Though being forgotten may make us profoundly unhappy, we do not perish when others forget us.

The neglect of being is a spiritual problem, that is, a problem of openness, an unwillingness to let fundamental questions and insights about one's existence emerge. One's being is mysterious, and an encounter with mystery can be uncomfortable if not threatening. That I am raises the question, How is it that I am? This is a question that points to dependence, and dependence upon some sort of First Cause is a burden to one's sense of independence and a diminishment of one's inflated idea of autonomy.

Being also escapes human control, and it is hard for us humans to accept limitations, especially limitations on what we think we possess. "To be or not to be" does not pose real options. People are, and they never asked to be. They may desire not to be but lack the courage to commit suicide. Or they may recognize that suicide does not guarantee nonbeing or release from suffering. A human being is stuck in being. However much we may pride ourselves on our mastery over self and world, we must admit, after pondering our existence, that a person's being determines his or her limits. We must conform to our being; one's being is master.

Awareness that one is carries with it awareness of dependence and limitation. Such awareness of one's being increases awareness of the being of all other things. Things in turn carry with them reminders of interdependence and limitation. The universe of being balks at an egoistically inflated sense of autonomy and control. Forgetfulness of one's being helps to protect a person from the uncomfortable acceptance of limitation and dependence.

To accept that one exists independent of other minds, that one has an origin in a line of causation, that consciousness of self follows one's being — is to acknowledge a foundation for personal existence and identity far more stable than one's ever-changing thoughts.

This long exposition of ignorance of being is designed to make concrete what remains an intuition of being. Intuition of being is for Merton, the underlying experience for appreciating the Christian doctrine of creation. (p. 220) To intuit the wonder of existing is to intuit one's contingency and, hence, one's origin in divine love. But what of Merton's assertion that ignorance of being, especially one's own, is a "root-sin" and that such ignorance leads to experiencing one's existence as a "disease"? The theological foundation of the above description of ignorance of being is that one's existence emerges from God's creative love. Merton, in *Conjectures of a Guilty Bystander*, recognizes this foundation in classical terms: "My act of being is a direct participation in the Being of God" (p. 221).

To be a gift is to be loved, to be in loving relationship, to be in a position to gratefully accept oneself as gift. To be outside of loving relationship, to be outside of gift, is to be in an unfriendly universe, a victim of impersonal forces. Such a person is inadequately defined because out of touch with his or her origin.

Unable to rest in the embrace of Being, humans look with anxiety for happiness elsewhere. In Merton's words, such people are always proclaiming that they stand "on frontiers of new abundance and permanent bliss" (ibid.).

When such dis-ease drives people to peer desperately across all frontiers for permanent bliss, they futilely attempt to create an impossible happiness; they fall into exteriority. Genuine happiness, according to Merton, consists in receiving self and reality as gifts, but people aren't home to receive gifts because they are outside, on Desolation Row, looking. Merton says that

> it is precisely this illusion, that mechanical progress means human improvement, that alienates us from our own being and our own reality. It is precisely because we are convinced that our life, as such is better if we have a better car, a better TV set, better toothpaste, etc. that we condemn and destroy our own reality and the reality of our natural resources. Technology was made for man, not man for technology. In losing touch with being and thus with God, we have fallen into a senseless idolatry of *production*

and *consumption* for their own sakes. . . . We no longer know how to live, and because we cannot accept life in its reality, life ceases to be a joy and becomes an affliction. And we even go so far as to blame God for it! (p. 222)

Merton does not believe technology is immoral[17] but, rather, that those who lose touch with being, with themselves and God, expecting from technology a happiness it cannot give, will espouse productivity and consumption as sacraments of salvation. He offers social criticism, but Merton's criticism is rooted in an analysis of a problem of ignorance of origin from, and relationship with, God.

When people believe increased technological progress and/or increased production and consumption will mean human improvement, they believe more is better. When more is better, people take a quantitative approach to life. Instead of relating technological production to meeting genuine human ends, people become subject to the rule of the technological system, spending their lives on an assembly line in order to consume things they don't need. Merton says that in this sort of dehumanization, a person

> becomes on one side an implement, a "hand," or better, a "bio-physical link" between machines: on the other side he is a mouth, a digestive system and an anus, something *through which* pass the products of his technological world, leaving a transient and meaningless sense of enjoyment.[18]

Illusion of autonomy

TO BE OUT OF TOUCH WITH BEING, which implies ignorance of one's relationship with God, Merton understands to be the source of technological madness and ecological irresponsibility. Such social issues he sees rooted in the illusion that the human self is completely morally autonomous. He says, in *Conjectures*, that

> to start with one's ego-identity and to try to bring

> that identity to terms with external reality by thinking, and then, having worked out practical principles, to act on reality from one privileged autonomous position — in order to bring it into line with an absolute good we have arrived at by thought: this is the way we become irresponsible. If reality is something we interpret and act on to suit our own concept of ourselves we "respond" to nothing. (p. 265)

To be living within this self-centered bubble is to adjust perception to one's desires. To screen out the world God has made in order to live in the mental world made by self, where one rules as God, is the moral root of social disorder (see pp. 224, 339). This self of clear and distinct ideas, Descartes' thinking subject, is a self alienated from its origin.

At various places in the text Merton calls this superficial ego "a cramp," a word that suggests a painful and knotted tightness. This cramp comes from living in fear of reality that may ask one to grow. This cramp of a self is one's self-willed identity rather than one's God-willed identity. This cramp is the effort of the individual to exist by willfully affirming self in opposition to everything else in order to distinguish the self. The cramp is the rejection of every reminder of one's dependence, contingency, giftedness (p. 224).

Complete moral autonomy, like the illusion of productivity and consumption as salvific, derives from an ignorance of one's relatedness to God.

Return to God

MERTON'S SOLUTION to this "root-sin" is to return to God in Christ:

> The basic Christian faith is that he who renounces his delusive, individual autonomy in order to receive his true being and freedom in and by Christ is "justified" by the mercy of God in the Cross of Christ. . . . Instead of my own delusive autonomy I surrender to Christ all rights over me in the hope that

by His Spirit, which is the Spirit and Life of His Church, He will live and act in me, and, having become one with Him, having found my true identity in Him, I will act only as a member of His Body and a faithful citizen of His Kingdom. (p. 115)

Reception of the gift of faith involves renunciation of former ways of being and self-understanding. By surrendering to Christ the completely morally autonomous self, one may experience life as interpenetration of the divine and human, where divine and human centers coincide. Thus one's point of reference is shifted from one's fulfillment and satisfaction to realization of the mystery of Christ as part of His Mystical Body (p. 114).

To receive the gifts of God, one must die to the image of a completely autonomous self. The notion of receptivity applies also to the illusory quest for happiness through mindless devotion to production and consumption. What Merton believes people need is love and a meaningful life (p. 224), which cannot be produced by even the most sophisticated technology. To be able to receive, one must go beyond will power to grateful acceptance of dependence.

The cramp of the self, which is developed by opposing reality in order to establish and maintain itself, must relax.[19] This relaxation comes by consciously accepting the fact that one already is established by God in His loving creativity. Instead of trying to exist by saying no to everything else in order to distinguish oneself,[20] one must say yes to God's prior yes:

> If we take a more living and more Christian perspective we find in ourselves a simple affirmation which is not of ourselves. It simply *is*. In our being there is a primordial *yes* that is not our own; it is not at our disposal; it is not accessible to our inspection and understanding.
>
> ... my being is not an affirmation of a limited self, but the "yes" of Being itself, irrespective of my own choices. Where do "I" come in? Simply in uniting the

"yes" of my own freedom with the "yes" of Being that already *is* before I have a chance to choose. . . . There is the actuality of one "yes." In this actuality no question of "adjustment" remains and the ego vanishes. (p. 266)

The yes to God's affirmation is faith, is entrance into the world He creates and rules. Such entrance entails the gradual relaxation of one's defensive posture so that one has a greater capacity to receive love and meaning. This shift in horizon Merton calls taking "a more living and Christian perspective."

This personalist reading of the social issue implied in living in a technological society is meant to illustrate Merton's underlying concern for the person. This reading of *Conjectures* further supports the contention that the root insight of Merton into the person brings unity to his thought; in this case, to his social criticism.

Oriental Spirituality

AS MERTON'S SOCIAL CONCERN SPANS his entire adult life, so, too, does his interest in Oriental wisdom. The first monk Merton ever met was an Oriental. Bramachari, a Hindu, had been living in America for several years when Merton met him. Bramachari visited one of Merton's friends, Seymour, during Merton's days at Columbia University.[21] Around this time, Merton had been reading books on Oriental mysticism, an interest sparked by his reading of Aldous Huxley's *Ends and Means*.

After his conversion to Catholicism, Merton for a time looked down upon non-Christian religion,[22] but his interest in Oriental spirituality continued throughout his adult life despite his temporary narrow-mindedness. Already in 1946, Merton's interest in Buddhist contemplative experience is apparent.[23] By 1959, in "The Inner Experience," he writes of Zen enlightment in very positive terms.[24]

At the end of his life, Merton was telling Cistercian and Benedictine superiors to learn from Oriental traditions of spirituality.[25]

Among the books Merton owned and which are now stored in the Merton Room in the Abbey of Gethsemani, one sees his major Oriental interests: Buddhism — especially Zen — Hinduism, and Chinese religion. He wrote numerous articles and several books on oriental spirituality, including *Mystics and Zen Masters, The Way of Chuang Tzu, Zen and the Birds of Appetite,* and *Gandhi on Non-Violence.*

In Merton's Oriental writings, there are two principal sources of his personalism: books and articles about Oriental topics (including articles and introductions for Oriental readers) and autobiographical references. The autobiographical materials reveal Merton's interest in the area of Oriental spirituality. Of these materials, *The Asian Journal* is the most fertile source.

There is, however, a temptation to simplify the man's complex development into clear spiritual stages. For example, to a certain extent, the dynamic of withdrawal and return fits Merton's life. Robert Giannini has applied Toynbee's model of disengagement, withdrawal, and return to Merton.[26] He does this in order to disclose patterns for a theoretical understanding of spiritual development. Unfortunately, squeezing Merton into such a pattern may imply that the withdrawal dynamic ends as the mature Merton reaches out into contemporary social commentary and interreligious dialog.

Presumably the mature Merton went to the Orient, not only to talk, but also to listen. *The Asian Journal* shows Merton to be concerned about spiritual progress; he remains to the end a spiritual seeker. In *The Asian Journal,* Merton receives advice from a tibetan lay monk about the advisability of learning from a guru. Merton showed an openness to this advice: "Why not?" he says (p. 42). In the opening entry in *The Asian Journal,* Merton, ever the seeker, quietly dedicates his trip to the Orient: "May I not come back without having settled the great affair" (p. 4). "The great affair" is the quest for God and his long study of oriental religion.

In *The Asian Journal,* Merton's focus is on spiritual liberation (pp. 56, 90, 96, 105, 111), spiritual practice and experience (pp. 68, 95, 104, 135, 316), and identity and enlightenment (pp. 68, 95, 104, 135, 316). These concerns would surprise only those unfamiliar with Merton or those who have imagined him to be turned to the world's problems *instead* of his monastic quest. One would expect any genuine contemplative seeker to share these interests.

The Subject-Object Split

DESIRING TO OVERCOME the subject-object split in his relationship with God, Merton recognizes a corresponding interest in certain Oriental teachings. Exploration of this aspect of Merton's dialog with Oriental spirituality will clarify a dimension of his personalism: that his personalism is compatible with the language and experience of self (self-concerned ego) and, furthermore, that the vanishing of self-concerned ego allows for the nondual experience of God as ultimate mind. Merton's personalism is not compatible with subject-object categories as he understands them. Additionally, otherness may or may not be present in authentically personal experience of God.

Merton's descriptions of Cartesian consciousness help us to understand what he means by transcending consciousness of subjects versus objects. While Merton does not strictly define *subject* or *object*, he describes Cartesian consciousness, in *Zen and the Birds of Appetite*, as

> a subject for whom his own self-awareness as a thinking, observing, measuring and estimating "self" is absolutely primary.... The more he is able to develop his consciousness as a subject over against objects, the more he can understand things in their relations to him and one another, the more he can manipulate these objects for his own interests, but also at the same time, the more he tends to isolate himself in his own subjective person, to become a detached observer cut off from everything else. . . .
> (p. 22)

Merton's key words describing Cartesian consciousness are "over against," "isolate," "detached observer." All of these terms are connected with the idea of the primacy of self-concern. This Cartesian consciousness heightens subject-object awareness by isolating self from others through self-reflexive concern. Merton contrasts this self-centered consciousness with what both "Oriental religions and Christian mysticism have stressed," namely, that the self-aware subject is provisional: "Its existence has meaning insofar as it does not become fixated or centered upon itself as ultimate, learns to function not as its own center but 'from God' and 'for others'" (p. 24). Thus Merton reaches for relational language ("from God" and "for others") in order to contrast with subject and object language.

Merton also contrasts Cartesian consciousness with the word *immediate.* He speaks (pp. 23, 24) of an "immediate experience of Being" that is beyond awareness of objects, especially of oneself as an object. The immediacy of "pure consciousness" rather than "consciousness of" leads Merton to speak in negative language, such as of the subject's disappearing (p. 24).

The connection between immediacy and disappearance of the subject is not so mysterious as to be beyond ordinary discourse. Two people in love, for example, are sympathetically present to each other and to the variety of expressions of the other, including feelings, gestures, and speech. They are not assuming the interior posture of detached observers. Their presence to each other in love would be diminished by detached, hence relatively distant, observation and further diminished by reflections on the self.

Similarly, one may experience God in a sympathetic immediacy or as a distant object "over against" one's self-concerned ego. One's self-concern disappears to the degree that one is attentive to the other.

Thus self-concern is synonymous with subject-object split, or Cartesian consciousness. The categories of subject and object imply a split, which is to say a separation, or distance, between subject and object. In Merton's understanding, the language of self disappearing refers to self in communion:

> Is a personal encounter with a personal God limited to an experience of God as "object" of knowledge and love on the part of a clearly defined, individual, and empirical subject? Or does not the empirical self vanish in the highest forms of Christian mysticism?[27]

Here, in *Mystics and Zen Masters*, Merton tries to remind his Christian readers of a personal encounter with God that is beyond categories of subject and object.

In the last weeks of his life, Merton catches himself falling into alienation on his hectic Asian pilgrimage. In the Himalayas, Merton took time to be quiet on the Mim tea estate. His thought is expressed in short bursts:

> Reassessment of this whole Indian experience in more critical terms. Too much movement. Too much "looking for" something: an answer, a vision, "something other." And this breeds illusion. Illusion that there *is* something else. Differentiation — the old splitting-up process that leads to mindlessness instead of the mindfulness of seeking all-in-emptiness and not having to break it up against itself.[28]

Even the fervent seeker is not immune to religious alienation. If the quest for transcendence is engineered by a Cartesian thinking subject,[29] the journey will be aborted. The self watching itself purify itself, though possessing many spiritual things, remains separated from the sought transcendence. In Zen, Merton finds articulation of this insight of transcending the subject-object split, and he writes of this in both *Mystics and Zen Masters* and *Zen and the Birds of Appetite*.[30]

In *Mystics and Zen Masters*, Merton sees Hui Neng as the great teacher of this nondual truth. Hui Neng opposed the approach to Zen that includes self-conscious self-purification. The ego achievements of self-purification interfere with true enlightenment. Merton understands Hui Neng's view of consciousness as the "ultimate mind" being manifested through the empirical self (p. 24). "We cannot be enlightened by cutting the manifestation off from the original light and giving it an autonomous existence which it cannot possibly have (p. 25).

Instead of the empirical ego enthroned at the center of a spiritual project of attainment, Merton understands Hui Neng's type of Zen as a way of "self-forgetfulness," a way to step out of the way of the ultimate mind, or *"prajna,"* which Merton understands in Christian terms as God: "We now know ourselves not in ourselves, not in our own mind, but in *prajna*, or as a Christian would say, in God" (p. 27). Thus Merton affirms transcendence of the subject-object split as compatible with "personal encounter with a personal God" (p. 29). Instead of God as an object that is objectively present, Merton finds in Zen writings confirmation of experience of God as center of one's center, as one's true self.

While the personalism of Walsh and Merton allows for nondual Christian experience, Merton does not deny the validity of Christian experience that relates to God as other. During Merton's last days in the United States, he answered Brother David Steindl-Rast, OSB, who asked him about intercessory prayer when both were at Our Lady of the Redwoods Trappistine Monastery in California:

> We are not rainmakers, but Christians. In our dealings with God he is free and so are we. It's simply a need for me to express my love by praying for my friends; it's like embracing them. If you love another person, it's God's love being realized. One and the same love is reaching your friend through you, and you through your friend.

Brother David asked if this type of prayer does not express a dualism, but Merton responds:

> Really there isn't, and yet there is. You have to see your will and God's will dualistically for a long time. You have to experience duality for a long time until you see it's not there. In this respect I am a Hindu. Ramakrishna has the solution. Don't consider dualistic prayer on a lower level. The lower is higher.

There are no levels. Any moment you can break through to the underlying unity which is God's gift in Christ. In the end, Praise praises. Thanksgiving gives thanks. Jesus prays. Openness is all.[31]

Merton maintains I-Thou experience as well as pure immanence as dimensions of personalism. In his earlier *Mystics and Zen Masters*, he associates the nondual experience with "the highest forms of Christian mysticism."[32] In 1968, in a conversation with Brother David, he recognizes that dualistic prayer is not "on a lower level.... Openness is all."[33] However one finds God, the connection is what matters. Personal relatedness with God, in Merton's understanding, thus would not necessarily imply a subject-object distinction. Yet to maintain the language of person while describing the process of allowing divine subjectivity to manifest itself through one's human subjectivity points to the need in the aspirant to unfold or make available the deepest treasure of one's experience of self. In other words, omission of person language might denigrate the dialogical forms of prayer. Maintaining person language allows for I-Thou type of conscious relationship, and because of the person-versus-individual, or true-versus-false-self dialectic, the reader of person language is protected from mistaking person for that which needs to be renounced.

Zen Experience

ZEN FASCINATED MERTON, and his respect and admiration for Zen as a way of life led him to defend it against Western misinterpretations. His method of defense makes use of person as his underlying insight, or root metaphor. In *Mystics and Zen Masters*, Merton notes mistaken Western descriptions of Zen as individualism, subjectivism, pantheism. He dismisses these clichés as "useless" (p. 17), principally because of insufficient understanding, since Buddhist and Zen concepts do not always find translatable equivalents in Western metaphysics. Rather than trying to fit Zen into an abstract philosophical system, Merton recognizes that Zen language derives from "concrete spiritual experience" (p. 16).

Merton does not so much try to translate Western concepts into Zen language as to find in Zen resonances of his own central concern. The language he uses to express these resonances is that of the personalism of Walsh and himself. Merton bemoans the failure of Western culture to distinguish between empirical ego and the person (p. 17). Such failure has contributed to a false understanding of Zen. Does not the Zen "no self" sound like the antithesis of any personalism? The Westerner who thinks of "no self" as depersonalizing confuses the superficial self with the person.

Merton does not give the Western reader a lexicon of Zen terms. Rather he acknowledges the linguistic poverty of Zen and points to the sought experience in Zen, which he expresses in his own personalistic terms. The linguistic poverty in Zen, he says in *Mystics and Zen Masters*, is that "the explicit concept of person in the highest sense is unfortunately absent" (p. 18). The importance of this quotation is that it identifies Merton's root metaphor as personalistic in the Walshian sense, from which he sympathetically and respectfully criticizes and defends Zen.

The sought experience in Zen, Merton expresses in the terms worked out between himself and Walsh:

> It is a recognition that the whole world is aware of itself in me, and that "I" am no longer my individual and limited self, still less a disembodied soul, but that my "identity" is to be sought not in that *separation* from all that is, the denial of my own personal reality, but its highest affirmation. (Ibid.)

Thus Merton chooses the language of person in order to explain Zen to Western readers. He uses person language because it has most adequately expressed his own spiritual experience. We may also say that he uses person language in the face of Western misunderstanding of ego and person in order to deepen the meaning of person in his largely Western readership.

Beneath the diversity in Merton's interests in social issues,

Oriental thought, and spiritual life lies an underlying insight. This insight Merton discusses when he expresses his concerns through writing. In order to deal with the complexity of historical realities, Merton employes principles deriving from a person-centered view of life. Merton also relates the challenge of Oriental thought on spirituality to person language. In this latter work, Merton protects the heights of spiritual experience from the deadening effect of the impersonal. The many-sided Merton has a center.

NOTES FOR CHAPTER V

1. Stephen C. Pepper, "Search for the Root Metaphor," in *A Modern Introduction to Metaphysics*, ed., D.A. Drennan (New York: The Free Press, 1962), p. 267.
2. Furlong, *Merton: A Biography*.
3. See, for example, Gerald Twomey, ed., *Thomas Merton: Prophet in the Belly of a Paradox* (New York: Paulist Press, 1978), pp. 92-110; Baker, *Thomas Merton, Social Critic*, pp. 27-65; Malits, *Solitary Explorer*, pp. 75-97.
4. Furlong, p. 256.
5. Malits, *Solitary Explorer*, pp. 84-85; see also Merton, *The Secular Journal* (New York: Farrar, Straus & Giroux, 1959), p. ix.
6. *SJ*, p. 322.
7. Merton, *My Argument with the Gestapo* (New York: New Directions, 1969), p. 77.
8. See *SJ*, p. 333; *NS*, pp. ix, x; and Malits, pp. 86-91.
9. *SJ*, p. 334.
10. *NVA*, pp. 20-62.
11. It was first published in the May 1967 edition of the magazine *Fellowship*; reprinted in July 1967 in pamphlet form by the Catholic Peace Fellowship; reprinted in 1968 in Merton's *Faith and Violence* (University of Notre Dame Press); reprinted again in *Thomas Merton on Peace* (New York: McCall, 1971); the revised edition of which is *The Nonviolent Alternative*, which is quoted in this chapter.
12. *NVA*, p. 209.
13. Merton's call for nonviolence does not imply what he calls "pure pacifism," as he admits the possible legitimate use of force. See *NVA*, p. 187.
14. Jacques Maritain, *A Preface to Metaphysics* (New York: Sheed and Ward, 1948), p. 48. This book was first published in 1939.
15. *CGB*, p. 220.
16. *CGB*, p. 222.
17. *LL*, pp. 69, 152.
18. *CGB*, pp. 76-77.
19. Another way Merton expresses the cramp and its remedy is that people operate under the illusion that unless they create an identity out of their work, they will fall into nothingness; see James H. Forest, "Thomas Merton's Struggle with Peacemaking," in *Thomas Merton: Prophet*, Twomey, ed., pp. 52-53. The remedy amounts to humility, or becoming lost to oneself to be found by God; see "Gelassenheit" in Merton's *Collected Poems*, p. 452.
20. *CGB*, p. 224.

21. *SSM*, pp. 190-195.

22. "Ultimately, I suppose all Oriental mysticism can be reduced to techniques that do the same thing, but in a far more subtle and advanced fashion: and if that is true, it is not mysticism at all. It remains purely in the natural order. That does not make it evil, *per se*, according to Christian standards: but it does not make it good, in relation to the supernatural. It is simply more or less useless, except when it is mixed up with elements that are strictly diabolical. . . ." *SSM*, p. 185; see also Thomas Merton, *Exile Ends in Glory* (Milwaukee: Bruce, 1948), p. 142.

23. Merton, *Mystics and Zen Masters* (New York: Farrar, Straus & Giroux, 1967) pp. 7-8. Cited hereafter as *MZM*.

24. *IE*, pp. 5-7. There Merton offers a description of Zen experience from classical Buddhist literature to illustrate spiritual awakening for his Christian readers.

25. *AJ*, p. 343.

26. Robert Giannini, "Model for Assessing Merton's Significance," *Cistercian Studies*, 13:4 (1978), pp. 379-383.

27. *MZM*, pp. 29-30.

28. *AJ*, p. 148.

29. See MZM, p. 26; *ZBA*, p. 22.

30. *MZM*, especially, pp. 18-34; *ZBA*, especially pp. 71-88.

31. David Steindl-Rast, "Man of Prayer," in *Thomas Merton, Monk*, ed. Patrick Hart (New York: Sheed and Ward, 1974), pp. 88-89.

32. *MZM*, p. 26.

33. Steindl-Rast, p. 89.

VI

SIGNIFICANCE FOR CHRISTIAN THOUGHT

WHAT IS THE SIGNIFICANCE for Christian thought of the notion of the person according to Walsh and Merton? In a sentence, it is that they revitalize the notion of the person with the meaning of image of God.

Person versus Nature

DISCUSSION OF THE PERSON according to Walsh may begin with the Boethian definition, "individual substance of a rational nature." To try to understand a person as a type of substance is to categorize, an activity consistent with the work of Aristotle. To understand a person as a type of substance is to distinguish persons from other types of beings and, thereby, to determine how persons fit into a hierarchy of beings.

In contrast with the view of person as a type of substance or in terms of how persons fit into a hierarchy of beings, Walsh and Merton understand the person as essentially a being in relationship with God. Person originates in, is guided by, and is called to union with, God. This view of person expresses a religious activity that links person with God rather than the activity of categorization that locates persons within an order of being. To link person with God is consistent with the image-of-God traditions of biblical and also Platonized Christianity.

When Merton and Walsh refer to a type of substance, they use the term *nature* rather than *person*. Both Walsh and Merton emphasize that an approach to the human in terms of "human nature" yields *what* a human being is. What a human person is may be encapsulated in such metaphysical definitions as Boethius's or Richard of St. Victor's "incommunicable existence." Even Thomas Aquinas's approach, the psychological sensitivity of which adds the note "center of action" to the understanding of person, still yields only the *what* of person. But as Walsh and Merton stress, *what* a person is, is not *who* that person is.

The *who* of personal existence is constituted by relationship. Both Walsh and Merton are too involved with ultimacy to say that who one is, is determined primarily by relationship with other human beings. Who one is, in the deepest sense, is a function of relationship with God. One's origin, way, and end are determined by relationship with God.

Though contrasting person with nature helps us understand person, there is a danger in such contrast. The danger of speaking of nature versus person is that one's discourse may become unduly abstract. There is no person apart from nature; person and nature are not two separate beings!

It is possible to emphasize the contrast between person as a type of substance and person as image of God, but the relationship between these two understandings of person need not be characterized as antagonistic. One may take an inclusive approach, joining the view of person as individual substance of rational nature with the religious view of relationship with God. Combining these views, one is led to look into the depths of the meaning of rational nature. To be rational in a religious sense is to apply one's intelligence to ultimacy: to one's origin, way, and end.

This dimension of ultimacy, or transcendence, is precisely what Walsh and Merton, in their inclusive and irenic approach, want to bring out. They do not jettison Aristotelian language or all language derived from efforts to categorize beings in a hierarchy. They use the term *nature*, for example, when talking about the order of beings. They are at home with the language of classical metaphysics, as is evidenced by their references to nature, being, and causality.

What Walsh and Merton accomplish is an infusion of religious meaning into the word *person*, which had nearly lost its transcendent dimension. They take a word that the Scholastic theologians use and bring to it new religious vitality from the image-of-God traditions. Some of that vitality can be thematized in terms of contingency, exemplarity, and finality.

Contingency

THOMAS MERTON SPEAKS of his deepest identity as being loved by God. He refers to intuition of his own being in terms of intuiting God's holding him in being. Merton thus emphasizes human contingency in his discussion of human identity. This stress upon efficient causality, however, does not answer the question of how persons differ from other beings.

Though person and nature are distinguishable, they are not separable in existence. Hence reference to nature enables one to distinguish between persons and other beings. Persons know and love; that is, persons are reflective and can love with a degree of freedom that lower beings cannot. Furthermore, those persons who are contingent may be conscious of their contingency and, hence, of their origin.

Exemplarity

WALSH, UNLIKE MERTON, points out that the notion of person does not necessarily refer to something contingent. Walsh's meaning of person thus applies to human, angelic, and divine persons. The preexistent Son images the Father, and all created persons image the Son.

Walsh sees persons as originating in God's incommunicable experience of Himself as imitable. Persons thus image, or imitate, God's own inner life. Merton also speaks in exemplaristic terms of persons when he says that human persons are words that echo His word and words that originate in His Word.

Finality

IN ADDITION TO SEEING PERSONS in terms of exemplarity, or as images of God, Walsh and Merton focus upon persons as called by God to union with Him. In other words, Walsh and Merton see the person in terms of finality. The person is the actualization of God's intention to perfect created persons or to restore fallen persons to their likeness to the perfect Image of God.

Whether one refers to efficient causality, exemplarity, or finality in discussion of person, what Merton and Walsh emphasize is that persons originate in, are guided by, and are oriented to God. That divine backdrop for persons affords them a foundation for identity that can free them to some degree from self-assertive efforts to establish themselves by stepping on others.

Thus what Walsh and Merton contribute is an emphasis in the understanding of person; that emphasis is on relationship with God, not on any particular human faculties or activities in isolation from relationship with God. Focusing upon relation as the meaning of person rather than on substance carries two advantages. First, as just noted, person is understood, not in isolation from God, but only in relation with Him. Second, the focus on relation gives a dynamic meaning to person. Person implies the call of God, a call originating in His experience of Himself as imitable, a call that guides one through life and to the finality intended by God.

Individuality versus Uniqueness

THE ISSUE OF INDIVIDUALITY again exposes the difference in the approaches of categorization and the religious activity of linking persons with God. Categorization attempts to arrive at the person by distinguishing persons from nonpersons. Engaging in the activity of discrimination in oneself heightens one's sense of individuality. However prized one's individual characteristics may be, if they are not related to God, they can interfere with the realization of one's personhood.

In approaching one's individual existence by linking self with God, one may image God through one's uniqueness. *Uniqueness* is the term for the positive aspect of individual existence. But individuality in isolation carries the danger of egoism. Uniqueness expresses the unrepeatable gift that each person is.

The chief danger for spirituality in the personalism of Walsh and Merton is the denigration of human individuality. Such denigration would be at odds with Christian teachings on the goodness of all creation (efficient causality), the plurality of divine Persons (exemplarity), and the divine call to created persons (finality).

Individual existence need not be placed in opposition to the person. The pejorative connotation that individuality consistently has in the thought of Walsh and, occasionally, in Merton expresses their recognition that self-centered living is at odds with the life that God intends. Merton notes that individuality can express one's personhood. Both Merton and Walsh allow the term *uniqueness* to describe the person. One may see in uniqueness the likeness to divine incommunicability in human persons.

Challenges to Identity

I BELIEVE THE REASON THAT Merton and Walsh do not focus on human nature or individuality in their understanding of person is the exigency for transcendence in their thought. That personhood is not contained totally in particular activities of human nature can be confusing for the student of Walsh and Merton, but that confusion is an effect of the challenge that their thought offers. Their challenge is on the level of identity. The identity called for is not an object in nature but rather a relationship with God. This issue of identity is the element in their thought that is most fruitful for spirituality.

Though transcendence is part of the understanding of person, distance is not thereby implied. *Person*, in the writings of Walsh and Merton, implies immediacy and directness, while *nature* implies abstraction and object knowledge. This note of immediacy is as important to Christian spirituality as is transcendence. Personal knowledge of God is not object knowledge; personal knowledge of God is prayer. Persons originate in, are guided by, and are fulfilled in a loving relationship with God. Walsh and Merton do not reject all object knowledge, but they invest their interest in personal knowledge of God.

Ordinarily — that is, outside of Christological and Trinitarian thought — the person is assumed to be synonymous with the individual. When Merton and Walsh make a point of distinguishing between person and individual, our comfort in this ordinary assumption is disturbed. A similar effect is engendered by Merton's reference to true versus empirical self. For one who assumes that there is only a single, everyday self, Merton's reference to two selves can initiate a line of questioning in search of true identity.

The quest for purification is also part of the spiritual journey. This journey culminates in transcendence, both in love of others and in contemplation of God. If human nature and human individuality are distinguished from the human person, the reason is to point toward the transcendence available to those who enter into the process of losing themselves to find themselves. The challenge to identity that Walsh and Merton offer is the challenge of bringing into one's conscious life one's divine Source, Guide, and End. in other words, the spiritual journey involves grounding psychological identity in one's metaphysical identity.

Walsh's questioning of individuality additionally, may stimulate one to understand Christian community as rooted in the call of God beyond individual personality differences. To relate to others solely on the basis of personality is to ignore the deepest level in oneself and others. To relate to others as persons is to acknowledge God's relationship to them.

Critical Observations

THOUGH NEITHER WALSH NOR MERTON is a systematic theologian, they nevertheless express their spirituality in theological terms. They keep discussion of Christian experience in tension with theological language. Thus they avoid an overly psychologized spirituality on the one hand and a theology divorced from experience on the other. It is unfortunate that their theology does not reflect any of the efforts of post-Vatican II exegetes, biblical theologians, and systematic theologians in the area of Christology.

Merton and Walsh use a Logos Christology. In other words, they imply, nearly exclusively, a model of Christ as preexistent Word and Second Person of the Trinity. Their understanding of Christ appears to be derived from Chalcedonian, patristic, and medieval Trinitarian and Christological thought.

The perfect Image as Logos thus determines what human imaging will mean. The content of that imaging is reducible to "love," but such reduction does not allow for the historical richness of the humanity of Christ to shine through. In order to be fair to them, however, one needs to remember that neither was trained in critical study of the New Testament. Their primary theological formation comes from the great medieval masters.

Although Walsh and Merton do not reflect contemporary developments in Christology, their personalism is a powerful development within Christian thought. This power comes from the weight of traditional language, which they rejuvenate. *Person* and *nature* are technical terms that historically had been invoked to settle ancient Christological disputes. Merton and Walsh take the term *person*, which is one of Christianity's most precious terms, and use it in such a way as to resonate with image-of-God traditions of spirituality.

In Walsh and Merton, person becomes a living concept, something more than an ancient theological tool for use in controversy. Their meaning of *person* is also deeper than promoters of the values of the "me" generation would dare consider. *Person* thus is rescued from 4th-century debate, on the one hand, and from 20th-century hedonism on the other. The power of classical Trinitarian and Christological theology, as well as of popular culture, resides in this term, which Merton and Walsh offer to the contemporary Christian.

There is an ambiguity in the meaning of *person* for Walsh

and Merton that is both a weakness and a strength. Reading Walsh and Merton, one is uncertain about whether *person* should be capitalized or not. Does *person* primarily refer to God, the Logos, or to humans? As I have noted, person as person refers to relationship with God, and one needs to refer to the nature, or activities of a being, in order to understand whether a particular person is divine or human.

The strength in this ambiguity is in its evocative power. If one understands person in the Walsh and Merton sense, then in referring to humans as persons, the divine referent is evoked. Humans as persons means humans as originating from and oriented to God. God as person refers to God as communicating with Himself, and that communication, in light of Christian teaching on creation, implies God as imitable. Hence human persons are implied by the divine Person.

The other meaning of person is the one mystical Person into whom humans are incorporated; that is, the relationship of the Son to the Father is shared with humans. The divine and the human poles of personhood resonate in the word *person*. That the divine and human imply each other within the realm of relationship perfectly fits the Christian mysteries of Trinity, Incarnation, Mystical Body, and Deification.

Person in Inter-religious Dialog

THE PERSONALISM OF WALSH AND MERTON offers an insight and a language that are fruitful in dialog between Christianity and Hinduism and Zen. For the Christian engaged in such dialog, there is a tension between harboring a sympathetic understanding of another religious tradition and preserving one's own Christian identity. Christianity prizes the language of persons. God is personal and human persons image Him. Within personal relationships between humans and God, love seems to necessitate an otherness that constitutes lover and beloved.

Some Oriental spiritualities seek a nondualistic experience in which otherness is lost along with the realm of the personal. Walsh and Merton, in their notion of the person, affirm the spiritual dynamic of transcending ego-dominated living. This transcendent experience is a link to the Hindu interest in a higher self and with the Zen interest in exposing the illusory nature of ego-consciousness. Merton and Walsh offer this link through the powerful language of person. Their understanding of person is compatible with nondual religious experience, for person is beyond ordinary individual identity. Merton's point of reference in his dialog with Oriental spirituality is the person. Referring to the unfortunate lack of the concept of person in Zen, for example, he says that the Zen concept of no-self refers to the superficial rather than to the deeper self, or the person. Furthermore, the goal of Zen, Merton expresses in terms of identity. Thus when Merton engages in dialog with Oriental spirituality, he makes use of concepts from his own personalism, thus confirming that person is a unifying key to his thought.

Person in Social Issues

MERTON ALSO SPEAKS OF a person-centered orientation in his discussions of social issues. No longer content to offer random social criticism, Merton tries to ground his social criticism in theological principles. These principles reveal his underlying concern for persons, who, in Merton's opinion, deserve to be treated as if they were Christ. Merton's social comment expresses concern for persons who are threatened by impersonal collectivities. Persons, for example, are routinely viewed by technocrats as merely part of the production system. His vision of persons as images of God leads Merton to cry out against such a reductionist view of persons.

Whether writing about a life of prayer, Oriental spirituality, or social issues, Merton's underlying concern, his basic point of reference, is the person. Exposure to Walsh's personalism facilitates the discovery of that underlying concern.

BIBLIOGRAPHY

THE WORKS OF DANIEL CLARK WALSH

THE WORKS OF DANIEL CLARK WALSH consist of his doctoral dissertation, articles, tape recordings, and transcriptions of talks and dialogs. Since most of his material is unpublished and available only at the Abbey of Gethsemani, Trappist, Kentucky, the list below follows the index to papers in Walsh's file at Gethsemani. This list is roughly chronological, not alphabetical. Since a number of these papers are untitled, the following list adheres to the index in the file at Gethsemani, for the sake of efficiency and to aid other scholars. The author has taken the liberty of titling the sixth item below "Person and Community I" and the seventh "Person and Community II."

"The Metaphysics of Ideas according to Duns Scotus." Ph.D. dissertation. (Toronto: Medieval Institute, 1933.)

"Some Reflections on the Concept of Substance in Medieval Philosophy." *Proceedings of the American Catholic Philosophical Association* (1962):102-106.

Duns Scotus Lecture given at St. Mary's, Kentucky, 1964.

"Anselm and Duns Scotus on Faith and the Person." Paper presented at Catholic University of America, Washington, D.C., 1966.

"Some Intimations of the Person in the Noetic of Knowledge and Love in the Doctrines of St. Thomas and Duns Scotus." Paper presented at St. Meinrad's Abbey, St. Meinrad, Indiana, 1963.

"Person and Community I." Group discussion, Abbey of Gethsemani, Trappist, Kentucky, November 6, 1971.

"Person and Community II." Group discussion, Abbey of Gethsemani, Trappist, Kentucky, November 12, 1971.

"New Ideas against Background of Continuing Tendencies in Philosophical Thought." Chapter talk, Abbey of Gethsemani, Trappist, Kentucky (not dated).

Chapter talk, Abbey of Gethsemani, Trappist, Kentucky, September 2, 1965.

Chapter talk, Abbey of Gethsemani, Trappist, Kentucky, October 7, 1965.

Chapter talk, Abbey of Gethsemani, Trappist, Kentucky, January 1966.

Chapter talk, Abbey of Gethsemani, Trappist, Kentucky, February 1966.

Philosophy conference, Abbey of Gethsemani, Trappist, Kentucky, March 1966.

Philosophy conference, Abbey of Gethsemani, Trappist, Kentucky, April 1966.

Chapter talk, Abbey of Gethsemani, Trappist, Kentucky, April 1966.

Chapter talk, Abbey of Gethsemani, Trappist, Kentucky, May 1966.

"The Role of the Spiritual in the New Philosophy of the Person." Philosophy conference, Abbey of Gethsemani, Trappist, Kentucky, June 2, 1966.

Chapter talk, Abbey of Gethsemani, Trappist, Kentucky, September 1966.

"A Philosophical Meditation: The Person: Freedom and Leadership." Philosophy conference, Abbey of Gethsemani, Trappist, Kentucky, September 1966.

"Role of the Intellect in the Economy of Christian Wisdom." Philosophy conference, Abbey of Gethsemani, Trappist, Kentucky, 1964.

"Three Conferences: On the Philosophy of Man and Universal Society, St. Thomas on Personalism and Nature." Abbey of Gethsemani, Trappist, Kentucky (not dated).

"Being and the Existent in Duns Scotus and St. Thomas." Philosophy conference, Abbey of Gethsemani, Trappist, Kentucky (not dated).

Group discussion, Abbey of Gethsemani, Trappist, Kentucky, May 5, 1975.

"Theology of Mysticism." Group discussion, Abbey of Gethsemani, Trappist, Kentucky, May 8, 1975.

"Person and Nature in Augustine." Audio tape no. 72 of the "Merton Tapes." Abbey of Gethsemani, Trappist, Kentucky, September 3, 1963.

Series of sixteen cassette recordings of a course in medieval philosophy given by Walsh at Bellarmine College, available at the Abbey of Gethsemani, Trappist, Kentucky.

Holographic letter fragment from Walsh to Thomas Merton located in packet of Merton-Walsh correspondence, Merton Studies Center, Bellarmine College, Louisville, Kentucky (1958).

"Thomas Merton: The Sense of Mystery." *Saint John's University Off Campus Record*, vol. 9 (summer 1969), pp. 13-19.

ARTICLES AND TAPE ABOUT WALSH

BURNS, FLAVIAN. Audio cassette tape on Walsh, Abbey of Gethsemani, Trappist, Kentucky, August 28, 1976.

DISTEFANO, ANTHONY. "Dan Walsh's Influence on the Spirituality of Thomas Merton." *The Merton Seasonal*, vol. 5 (1980), pp. 4-13.

"Merton's Professor to Be Ordained a Priest at 60." *National Catholic Reporter*, 26 April 1967, p. 1.

BOOKS BY THOMAS MERTON

The Ascent to Truth (New York: Harcourt, Brace, 1951).

The Asian Journal of Thomas Merton (New York: New Directions, 1973).

Bread in the Wilderness (New York: New Directions, 1953).

The Climate of Monastic Prayer (Kalamazoo: Cistercian Publications, 1964).

The Collected Poems of Thomas Merton (New York: New Directions, 1980).

Conjectures of a Guilty Bystander (New York: Image Books, 1968).

Contemplation in a World of Action (New York: Image Books, 1973).

Contemplative Prayer (New York: Image Books, 1969).

Disputed Questions (New York: Farrar, Straus & Cudahy, 1960).

Exile Ends in Glory (Milwaukee: Bruce, 1948).

Faith and Violence (Notre Dame: University of Notre Dame Press, 1968).

Gethsemani: A Life of Praise (Trappist, Kentucky: Abbey of Gethsemani, 1966).

The Last of the Fathers (New York: Harcourt Brace, 1954).

Life and Holiness (New York: Image Books, 1964).

The Living Bread (New York: Farrar, Straus & Giroux, 1956).

Love and Living (New York: Bantam Books, 1980).

The Monastic Journey (New York: Image Books, 1977).

My Argument with the Gestapo (New York: New Directions, 1969).

Mystics and Zen Masters (New York: Farrar, Straus & Giroux, 1967).

The New Man (New York: Farrar, Straus & Giroux, 1961).

New Seeds of Contemplation (New York: New Directions, 1961).

No Man Is an Island (New York: Image Books, 1967).

The Nonviolent Alternative (New York: Farrar, Straus & Giroux, 1981).

Opening the Bible (Collegeville: Liturgical Press, 1970).

Raids on the Unspeakable (New York: New Directions, 1966).

Redeeming the Time (London: Burns and Oates, 1966).

Seasons of Celebration (New York: Farrar, Straus & Giroux, 1964).

The Secular Journal of Thomas Merton (New York: Farrar, Straus & Giroux, 1977).

Seeds of Contemplation (Norfolk: New Directions, 1949).

Seeds of Destruction (New York: Farrar, Straus & Giroux, 1964).

The Seven Storey Mountain (New York: Signet Books, 1948).

The Sign of Jonas (Harcourt Brace Jovanovich, 1979).

Silent Life (New York: Farrar, Straus & Giroux, 1957).

Spiritual Direction and Meditation (Collegeville: Liturgical Press, 1960).

Thomas Merton on Peace. Edited with an Introduction by Gordon C. Zahn (New York: McCall Publishing Co., 1971).

Thomas Merton on St. Bernard (Kalamazoo: Cistercian Publications, 1980).

A Thomas Merton Reader (Garden City: Image Books, 1974).

Thoughts in Solitude (New York: Farrar, Straus & Cudahy, 1958).

The Waters of Siloe (New York: Harcourt Brace Jovanovich, 1949).

The Way of Chuang Tzu (New York: New Directions, 1965).

Wisdom of the Desert (New York: New Directions, 1960).

Zen and the Birds of Appetite (New York: New Directions, 1968).

ARTICLES BY THOMAS MERTON

"Baptism in the Forest: Wisdom and Initiation in William Faulkner." In *Mansions of the Spirit*, pp. 17-44. Edited by G. A. Panichas (New York: Hawthorn Books, 1967).

"Clement of Alexandria." In *Clement of Alexandria: Selections from the 'Protreptikos,'* pp. 1-13, by Titus Flavius Clemens. (Norfolk, Conn.: New Directions, 1963).

"A Conference on Prayer, Calcutta, October 27, 1968." *Sisters Today*, vol. 41 (April 1970), pp. 449-456.

"Concerning the Collection in the Bellarmine College Library." In *The Thomas Merton Studies Center*, pp. 13-15, by Thomas Merton, John Howard Griffin, and Msgr. Alfred F. Horrigan; vol. I (Santa Barbara: Unicorn Press, 1971).

"Day of a Stranger." *Hudson Review*, vol. 10 (summer 1967), pp. 211-218.

"The Death of God, I: The Death of God and the End of History." *Theoria to Theory*, vol. 2 (1967), pp. 3-16.

Foreword to *Bernard of Clairvaux*, by H. Daniel-Rops (New York: Hawthorn Books, 1964).

"Gandhi and the One-Eyed Giants." An introduction in *Gandhi on Non-Violence*. Edited by Thomas Merton (New York: New Directions, 1964).

Introduction and Commentary to *The Plague*, by Albert Camus (New York: Seabury Press, 1968).

Introduction to *The City of God*, by St. Augustine (New York: The Modern Library, 1950).

Introduction to *The Monastic Theology of Aelred of Rievaulx*, by A. Hallier. (Spencer, Mass.: Cistercian Publications, 1969).

Introduction to *The Prison Meditations of Father Alfred Delp*, by Alfred Delp (New York: Herder and Herder, 1963).

Introduction to *The Soul of the Apostolate*, by Dom J. B. Chautard, OCSO (Trappist, Kentucky: Gethsemani Abbey, 1946).

"The Japanese Tea Ceremony." *Good Work*, vol. 32 (1969), pp. 6-7.

"Love and Person." *Sponsa Regis*, vol. 32 (September 1960), pp. 6-11.

Preface to *In Search of a Yogi*, by Dom Denys Rutledge (New York: Farrar, Straus & Co., 1962).

UNPUBLISHED MATERIALS BY THOMAS MERTON

"Collected Essays." 22 volumes, Abbey of Gethsemani, Trappist, Kentucky (not dated).

"The Inner Experience." Abbey of Gethsemani, Trappist, Kentucky (not dated).

"Notebook 1: Notes on the Contemplative Life: Especially from the Cistercian Fathers and the Augustinians in General." Merton Studies Center, Bellarmine College, Louisville, Kentucky, January 17, 1946, through Pentecost 1948.

"Notebook 2: Notes on the Contemplative Life. Vol. 2: Dogma in Relation to Contemplation." Merton Studies Center, Bellarmine College, Louisville, Kentucky, Feast of St. Lucy 1947-1956.

"Notebook 21." Merton Studies Center, Bellarmine College, Louisville, Kentucky, April-June 1966.

"Notebook 52." Merton Studies Center, Bellarmine College, Louisville, Kentucky (not dated).

"Notebook 59." Merton Studies Center, Bellarmine College, Louisville, Kentucky (not dated).

BOOKS ABOUT THOMAS MERTON

BAILEY, RAYMOND. *Thomas Merton on Mysticism* (New York: Doubleday, 1975).

BAKER, JAMES T. *Thomas Merton, Social Critic: A Study.* (Lexington: University Press of Kentucky, 1971).

_____. *Under the Sign of the Water Bearer* (Louisville: Love St. Books, 1976).

BREIT, MARQUITA. *Thomas Merton: A Bibliography* (Metuchen: The Scarecrow Press, 1974).

CAPPS, WALTER H. *Hope against Hope* (Philadelphia: Fortress Press, 1976).

CASHEN, RICHARD A. *Solitude in the Thought of Thomas Merton* (Kalamazoo: Cistercian Publications, 1981).

DELL'ISOLA, FRANK. *Thomas Merton: A Bibliography* (New York: Farrar, Straus & Cudahy, 1956).

FINLEY, JAMES. *Merton's Palace of Nowhere* (Notre Dame: Ave Maria Press, 1978).

FURLONG, MONICA. *Merton: A Biography* (New York: Bantam Books, 1980).

GRIFFIN, JOHN HOWARD. *A Hidden Wholeness: The Visual World of Thomas Merton* (Boston: Houghton Mifflin Co., 1970).

HART, PATRICK, Ed. *Thomas Merton, Monk: A Monastic Tribute* (New York: Sheed and Ward, 1974).

HIGGINS, JOHN J. *Thomas Merton on Prayer* (Garden City: Image Books, 1975).

KELLY, FREDERICK J. *Man before God: Thomas Merton on Social Responsibility* (New York: Doubleday, 1974).

LABRIE, ROSS. *The Art of Thomas Merton* (Fort Worth: Texas Christian University Press, 1979).

LENTFOEHR, SR. THERESE. *Words and Silence: On the Poetry of Thomas Merton* (New York: New Directions, 1979).

MALITS, ELENA. *The Solitary Explorer* (New York: Harper & Row, 1980).

MCINERNY, DENNIS. *Thomas Merton: The Man and His Work* (Kalamazoo: Cistercian Publications, 1974).

NOUWEN, HENRI. *Thomas Merton: Contemplative Critic* (New York: Harper and Row, 1981).

PADOVANO, ANTHONY T. *The Human Journey* (Garden City: Doubleday, 1982).

PATNAIK, DEBA, Ed. *A Merton Concelebration* (Notre Dame: Ave Maria Press, 1981).

PENNINGTON, M. BASIL, OCSO., Ed. *The Cistercian Spirit: A Symposium in Memory of Thomas Merton* (Spencer, Mass.: Cistercian Publications, 1970).

RICE, EDWARD. *The Man in the Sycamore Tree: The Good Times and Hard Life of Thomas Merton* (New York: Doubleday, 1970).

SHANNON, WILLIAM H. *Thomas Merton's Dark Path* (New York: Farrar, Straus & Giroux, 1981).

TWOMEY, GERALD, Ed. *Thomas Merton: Prophet in the Belly of a Paradox* (New York: Paulist Press, 1978).

WOODCOCK, GEORGE. *Thomas Merton: Monk and Poet* (New York: Farrar, Straus & Giroux, 1978).

ARTICLES AND DISSERTATIONS ABOUT THOMAS MERTON

BURNS, FLAVIAN. "Consciousness of God and His Purpose in the Life and Writings of Thomas Merton." *The Merton Seasonal*, vol. 4 (summer 1979), pp. 1-5.

DAVIES, SR. MARGARET. "Thomas Merton's Re-thinking of the Christian Monastic Life in the Light of the *Boddhisatvacarya* of Mahayana Buddhism." M.A. thesis, University of St. Michael's College, Toronto, 1973.

FOREST, JAMES H. "Merton's Peacemaking." *Sojourners*, vol. 7 (December 1978), pp. 13-18.

GIANNINI, ROBERT. "Model for Assessing Merton's Significance." *Cistercian Studies*, vol. 13 (1978), pp. 379-383.

HAWKINS, ANNE OLIVIA. "Archetypes in the Spiritual Autobiographies of St. Augustine, John Bunyan, and Thomas Merton." Ph.D. dissertation, University of Rochester, 1978.

HERGOTT, ALVIN W. "Thomas Merton and the Image of Man." M.A. thesis, University of Saskatchewan, 1971.

KILCOURSE, GEORGE A. "Incarnation as the Integrating Principle in Thomas Merton's Poetry." Ph.D. dissertation, Fordham University, 1974.

MALITS, ELENA. "Journey into the Unknown: Thomas Merton's Continuing Conversion." Ph.D. dissertation, Fordham University, 1974.

MILLER, SAMUEL G. "Zen in the Christian Consciousness of Thomas Merton." B.A. thesis, Duke University, 1975.

STEINDL-RAST, DAVID. "Man of Prayer." In *Thomas Merton Monk*, edited by Patrick Hart (New York: Sheed and Ward, 1974).

_____. "Recollections of Thomas Merton's Last Days in the West." *Monastic Studies*, vol. 7 (1969), pp. 1-10.

TEAHAN, JOHN FRANCIS. "A Dark and Empty Way: Thomas Merton and the Apophatic Tradition." *Journal of Religion*, vol. 58 (July 1978), pp. 263-287.

──────. "The Mysticism of Thomas Merton: Contemplation as a Way of Life." Ph.D. dissertation, Princeton University, 1976.

──────. "The Place of Silence in Thomas Merton's Life and Thought." *Journal of Religion*, vol. 61 (1981), pp. 364-383.

TOBIN, MARY LUKE. "Merton on Prayer: Start Where You Are." *Praying*, no. 1; supplement to *National Catholic Reporter*, October 14, 1983; pp. 11-16.

VELAMKUNNEL, JOSEPH, S.J. "Transcendental Experience of God according to Thomas Merton: a Comparative and Theological Study of Oriental and Christian Mysticism." Ph.D. dissertation, Gregorian University, 1975.

WERBLOWSKY, R. J. ZWI. "Mystics and Zen Masters." *Cistercian Studies*, vol. 13 (1978), pp. 318-321.

www.ingramcontent.com/pod-product-compliance
Lightning Source LLC
Chambersburg PA
CBHW050809160426
43192CB00010B/1690